A Bit of Appliqué

EASY PROJECTS WITH MODERN FLAIR

AMY STRUCKMEYER

Martingale®
Create with Confidence

dedication

For Henry and Eleanor, who inspire me every day
with their creativity and imagination

A Bit of Appliqué: Easy Projects with Modern Flair
© 2015 by Amy Struckmeyer

Martingale®
19021 120th Ave. NE, Ste. 102
Bothell, WA 98011-9511 USA
ShopMartingale.com

Printed in China
20 19 18 17 16 15   8 7 6 5 4 3 2 1

Library of Congress Cataloging-in-Publication Data
is available upon request.

ISBN: 978-1-60468-553-4

mission statement

Dedicated to providing quality products
and service to inspire creativity.

credits

PUBLISHER AND CHIEF VISIONARY OFFICER
Jennifer Erbe Keltner

EDITORIAL DIRECTOR
Karen Costello Soltys

DESIGN DIRECTOR
Paula Schlosser

ACQUISITIONS EDITOR
Karen M. Burns

PHOTOGRAPHER
Brent Kane

TECHNICAL EDITOR
Ellen Pahl

PRODUCTION MANAGER
Regina Girard

COPY EDITOR
Tiffany Mottet

COVER AND
INTERIOR DESIGNER
Adrienne Smitke

ILLUSTRATOR
Missy Shepler

SPECIAL THANKS
Martingale thanks Cassie Barden
and Jon LeCroy of Seattle, Washington,
for generously allowing the photography
of this book to take place in their home.

contents

INTRODUCTION	4
TOOLS + SUPPLIES	6
APPLIQUÉ TECHNIQUES	7
OTHER TECHNIQUES + TIPS	14

PROJECTS

Sound Waves Quilt	16
Retro Flower Tote	20
Seedpod T-Shirt	31
Sunny Day Patch	34
Garden Skirt	38
Prairie Blooms Throw Pillow	42
Petals Pot Holder and Trivet	46
Geometric Throw Pillow	52
Spot-On Coasters	56
Circles Baby Quilt	59
Polly the Penguin Softie	66
Directional Messenger Bag	73
Sewing Love Pouch and Pincushion	81
Easy as Pie Tea Towel	88
No. 2 Pencil Pouch	92

ACKNOWLEDGMENTS	96
ABOUT THE AUTHOR	96

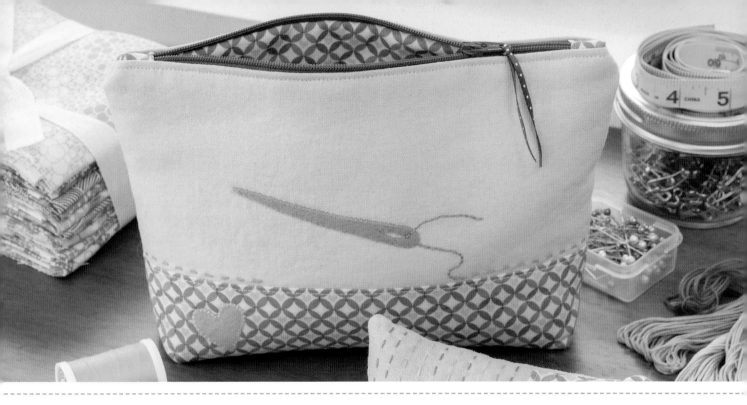

introduction

At it's very heart, this book is a collection of sewing projects. It contains patterns and instructions for sewing everyday items—for your home, for yourself or your child, or to give as gifts. There are useful and decorative items, and all are embellished with an appliqué design. Each project or pattern incorporates an appliqué technique, such as raw-edge fusible appliqué, reverse appliqué, or turned-edge appliqué prepared with freezer paper. There are projects featuring bias-tape appliqué, and one that uses quilted lines to secure appliqué shapes. Some of the designs include additional embellishments of embroidery, ribbon, or trim.

I hope this book provides enough variety—of project types, complexities, styles, and techniques—to appeal to you whether you're a beginner or more experienced sewist. I also hope you'll find new things to try, enjoy the experience, and make something (or some *things*) wonderful. And more than anything, I hope you'll find inspiration and encouragement here, to create your own unique variations on these designs, or maybe invent something altogether new!

WHY APPLIQUÉ?

Appliqué is full of possibilities, and it has the ability to transform an object. For example, take an ordinary tea towel or tote bag, embellish it with an appliqué design that means something to you (or to someone else) and you've turned that ordinary object into a unique, and perhaps even stunning, possession.

When I started designing sewing patterns, I was confident with a sewing machine, but I didn't have a lot of experience with complicated pattern construction. I could easily construct a throw pillow or a simple bag, for example, but not a detailed pieced front for the pillow, or a bag with many zippered pockets, flaps, etc. As an architect, I was good at picking apart a pattern and visualizing the whole two-dimensional or three-dimensional item, but I didn't feel like I was experienced enough to instruct others on complex pattern details. Beside, there were already plenty of other designers who could do that. So, looking for ways to make my patterns unique, I experimented with appliqué and other

▶ Quilting and appliqué can be combined, even in small projects such as this coaster.

▶ The simple, graphic nature of this paper sun collage inspired a scrappy fabric version.

embellishments, with a tendency for bold, graphic, and colorful designs. And when I looked for books on appliqué, to learn new techniques and gather inspiration and ideas, I found mainly books that focused specifically on quilting, with a fairly traditional style. This book is the one I wished I could have found then. As my sewing skills evolved, I found that I was sewing and designing more complex projects, but also continuing to add original embellishments, most often with appliqué.

Many of the projects in this book can stand on their own, and would look lovely sewn in a beautiful print, minus the appliqué, and so this is more than just a book about embellishment. All of the bags, the girl's skirt, and even the tea towel fall into this category. Yet other projects, such as the quilts, the coasters, the geometric throw pillow, and the stuffed penguin rely on appliqué as an inherent part of their design. While this book teaches techniques and provides project instructions, it's really intended to open your mind to limitless design possibilities.

INSPIRATION

Inspiration for appliqué designs is everywhere. I see possibilities in my garden, pictures in magazines, modern art, folk art, my kids' drawings—just about anywhere. Sometimes I'm inspired by a specific color combination or technique, but usually the design starts with an image and grows from there. Here are some ideas to get you started in creating your own appliqué designs. Remember, they don't need to be complicated. Sometimes simple is better.

Look at the artwork or drawings children make. There is often a beautiful simplicity to these, and a unique perspective. Children don't yet draw things the way we, as adults, have been ingrained to draw or "see" them.

Supersize a simple object or graphic, or make it really tiny.

Visit a museum, or just visit your local library and page through books full of paintings, prints, or woodcuts.

Go for a walk. Focus on really observing the things around you. Look at the shapes, color combinations, and patterns of natural and human-made things.

Introduction

tools + supplies

I sincerely believe you don't need a lot of fancy tools or expensive supplies for most sewing, and particularly for the projects in this book. That said, here is a list of some of the most necessary and helpful materials to get you started—and well on your way!

Sewing machine. A basic sewing machine with a few different stitches, including a zigzag stitch, is really all you need.

Presser feet. Besides a basic presser foot (one that allows for a wide stitch, such as a zigzag, as well as a straight stitch), a zipper foot is necessary for attaching zippers. A walking foot is helpful for sewing through multiple layers and quilting straight lines. A quarter-inch foot isn't necessary, but makes sewing consistent ¼" seam allowances in patchwork much easier.

Needles for hand and machine sewing. Use needles for your sewing machine that are appropriate for the type of fabric and thread you're using. The same is true for hand sewing. Use embroidery needles for embroidery (these are made for hand or machine sewing), finer needles for thinner fabric, and bigger needles for thicker fabric. Use sharp-pointed needles for woven fabrics, and rounded-tip (ballpoint) needles for knits so that the tip won't snag the knit.

Scissors. A pair of small, sharp scissors is essential for cutting tiny appliqué shapes, small slits, and notches, and is useful for clipping threads. Dressmaker shears are needed for larger cuts of fabric. And since cutting paper with your sewing scissors will make them dull quickly, you'll need one more pair of basic scissors for cutting anything that's not fabric!

Rotary cutter, mat, and clear acrylic ruler. If you choose to have only one ruler, I recommend a 6" x 24" ruler—it's long enough to cut a full width of fabric (when it's folded selvage-to-selvage). One smaller-sized ruler can also be useful for squaring up and cutting tinier fabric pieces.

Flexible measuring tape. Use this to measure objects that aren't flat, such as waistlines, and things that are longer than your 24" ruler.

Marking tools. An ultra-fine-tip permanent marker or graphite pencil is needed for tracing templates onto fusible web and freezer paper, among other things. You'll also need something for marking fabric. Use a blue water-soluble marker or colored chalk marker for lighter fabrics, and a light-colored water-soluble marker or chalk marker for dark fabrics. Just be sure to test any fabric marker or chalk on the fabric first to be sure it will disappear completely.

Pins and other temporary holders. Straight pins are a necessity; a safety pin is useful for feeding elastic through a casing; and binding clips are a bonus for holding multiple layers and bindings in place. In place of pins for holding a pattern piece in place, you can use pattern weights to save time.

Iron. Any iron with a pointed tip will do. A steam iron is a bonus, but you can also steam fabric with a hot, dry iron and a spritz of water from a spray bottle.

Pressing cloth. A thin, inexpensive cotton dish towel will do the trick. You don't want a terry cloth towel—just flat, woven cotton. It becomes a damp press cloth when you drench it with water, then ring out the excess. You'll need this for adhering fusible web and fusible interfacing.

appliqué techniques

Whether you like to appliqué by hand or machine, there are countless variations on each method. This book touches on just a few techniques that I like to use. All of the projects in this book can be either hand or machine appliquéd. I mostly prefer the latter because stitching by machine tends to be quicker and easier. However, handstitching works better for smaller pieces, and can be very soothing, meditative, and easily transportable.

Most of the projects in *A Bit of Appliqué* feature appliqué stitching that is visible, and in some cases, even a key element of the project, such as in the "Geometric Throw Pillow" on page 52 and the "Seedpod T-Shirt" on page 31. Other projects include additional machine stitching or hand embroidery to further enhance the design. See the "Prairie Blooms Throw Pillow" on page 42 and the "Garden Skirt" on page 38 for example.

My wish is that you will find something here that entices you. Perhaps you'll become more comfortable with an already familiar appliqué method or you'll be inspired to try something completely new.

MAKING A USABLE TEMPLATE OR PATTERN PIECE

Patterns are provided for all of the projects in this book, but how do you translate a shape on a page into something you can use to cut your fabric? There are several methods for making a usable template or pattern piece, without actually cutting up the pages of a book! Sometimes you can trace directly from a pattern onto fusible web. For other projects, I may recommend a specific method I feel works best in that particular case. Here are a few of the techniques I like to use for creating a template.

Paper patterns. Use a photocopy machine, or scanner and printer, to copy the pages that you need from the book. Cut the pattern from the copy paper. For patterns larger than one page,

▶ Hand stitching and embroidered details add a playful quality to the "Garden Skirt."

tape copy paper together along the match lines indicated on the pattern, and then cut it out. Pin the pattern to your fabric (or use pattern weights), and then cut around the shape.

Freezer-paper templates. Freezer paper is a plastic-coated paper originally made for wrapping and protecting frozen food. You can find it in rolls at some grocery stores, precut sheets (usually 8½" x 11") at many fabric stores and quilt shops, or in both forms online.

Lay freezer paper over a pattern in the book, with the dull side facing up. Trace the pattern and any important markings onto the freezer paper with a pencil or fine-point marker. Cut the shape from the freezer paper along the traced lines. With the shiny side of the freezer paper facing your fabric, iron the template to the fabric with a hot, dry iron. Then cut around the shape. The freezer paper will peel off easily, leaving no residue, and can be reused several times. Freezer paper is especially well suited to cutting felt appliqué shapes.

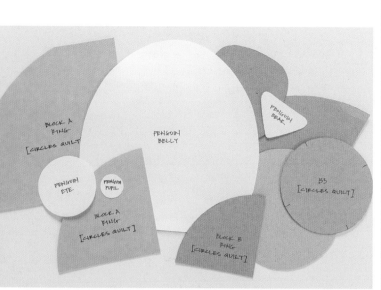

▶ Cardstock templates are handy and sturdy enough to be used many times.

▶ Raw-edge fusible appliqué is quick and easy. Here, a narrow zigzag stitch secures the edges.

Cardstock templates. Thin cardboard, chipboard, or cardstock from the recycling bin—empty cereal, pasta, or cracker boxes; used greeting cards; or document mailers—work great for creating templates you can use again and again. This is especially useful for small pattern pieces, or shapes you will need to trace many times. Follow these steps to make and use a cardstock template.

1 Trace the pattern in the book onto computer paper, tracing paper, wax paper, or any other paper through which you can see the shape; then cut out along the traced lines.

2 Lay the paper pattern on a piece of cardstock and carefully trace around the paper. Cut the shape from the cardstock.

3 Lay the cardstock template on your fabric or fusible web and trace around it with an appropriate marking instrument.

4 Cut along the traced marks or outside them, depending on the appliqué technique you are using.

Many people use template plastic or acrylic, and if you like those materials, by all means, use them! I use thin cardboard or cardstock simply because I almost always have some on hand, so I don't need to purchase it.

RAW-EDGE FUSIBLE APPLIQUÉ

This technique works for just about any shape and size. You'll apply fusible web to the wrong side of your appliqué fabric, cut out the shape, remove the paper backing, and fuse it to a background fabric. I use a lightweight fusible web, such as Pellon's Wonder-Under, so I can sew through the appliqué after it's been fused. This method is easy and quick—just follow the steps below.

1 Trace the pattern onto the paper side of fusible web with a pencil, pen, or permanent marker. You can make and trace a template or simply trace the pattern from the book pages. (If you're creating your own design, keep in mind that the shape will be reversed, or mirrored, when you're finished.) Cut out the shape, leaving roughly a ¼" border.

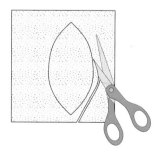

A Bit of Appliqué

3 Carefully remove the paper backing. Position the shape on the right side of the background fabric and fuse with your iron, following the manufacturer's instructions. Allow the appliqué to cool.

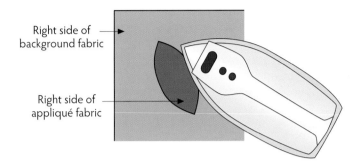

Right side of background fabric

Right side of appliqué fabric

4 Secure the raw edge of the appliqué by sewing it to the background fabric near the edge of the fused shape by hand or machine. Hand stitching or a straight machine stitch will allow woven fabrics to fray slightly at the edges over time. I like this look and use it often. To minimize the frayed look or to make the appliqué even more durable, use a narrow zigzag or satin stitch.

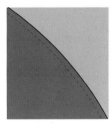

Straight stitch

2 Following the manufacturer's instructions, use your iron to fuse the shape to the wrong side of the appliqué fabric. Allow to cool, and then cut along the traced lines.

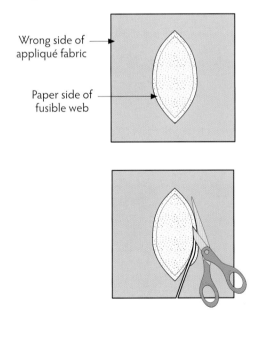

Wrong side of appliqué fabric

Paper side of fusible web

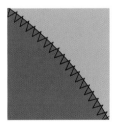

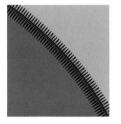

Narrow zigzag stitch   Satin stitch

▶ Since the raw edges won't fray, a simple straight stitch is all that's needed to hold wool felt appliqués in place.

▶ Multiple appliqué techniques can be combined in one project. The "Retro Flower Tote" (page 20) uses both turned-edge appliqué with freezer paper, and gathered-circle appliqué.

RAW-EDGE FELT APPLIQUÉ

This is the easiest technique in the book. Because the raw edges of wool felt will not fray, you just need to cut out your shape and sew it to the background.

1 Make a template by tracing the pattern onto the dull side of freezer paper. Cut it out along the drawn lines.

2 Iron the freezer-paper template to the felt and cut around it without adding any seam allowance.

3 Pin the felt shape to the background and stitch the raw edges by hand or machine. You can also cut a piece of fusible web, smaller than the pattern piece, and fuse it to the wrong side of the appliqué. Then fuse the appliqué to the background to hold it in place while you sew.

TURNED-EDGE APPLIQUÉ WITH FREEZER PAPER

With this method, you make a template with freezer paper and press the seam allowances of the appliqué over the freezer paper to the wrong side. It creates an appliqué with a clean, finished edge that won't fray, and works very well for gentle curves and straight-lined shapes. The resulting appliqués can be secured in place by hand or machine.

1 Trace the appliqué pattern onto the matte (not shiny) side of the freezer paper and cut out along the traced lines. Keep in mind that the final shape will be reversed or mirrored.

2 Place the freezer paper on the wrong side of the appliqué fabric, shiny side down, and iron it to the fabric with a hot, dry iron. This will temporarily attach the freezer paper to the fabric; you'll be able to peel the paper off later.

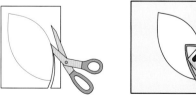

Wrong side of fabric

3 Cut the fabric, adding a ¼" seam allowance all around the paper shape, or as indicated on the pattern.

4 With the wrong side of the shape facing up, use a hot iron to press the raw edges of the fabric over the freezer-paper shape. Use a spray bottle of water or starch to dampen the seam allowances for easy pressing. You can also place the starch in a small container and paint it on the seam allowances with a small paintbrush. Press until the edges are smooth and the fabric is dry. Allow to cool.

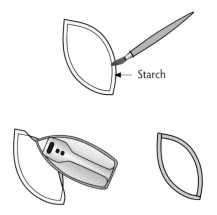

Starch

5 Carefully peel off the freezer paper, turn the shape right side up, and press the turned edges a final time.

6 Pin the shape in position on the background fabric and hand or machine stitch the shape in place. You can also cut a piece of fusible web smaller than the shape, adhere it to the wrong side of the appliqué, and fuse it to the background. This will hold it in place while stitching.

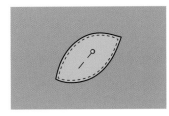

GATHERED-CIRCLE APPLIQUÉ

This method creates a circle with a turned edge. You can also use the "Turned-Edge with Freezer Paper" technique for similar results. Try both, and decide which method you prefer. I find the gathered method works best for pieced circles, thicker fabrics, and small circles.

1 Create a template of cardstock using the circle pattern provided.

2 Trace the template on the wrong side of the appliqué fabric and cut the circle ¼" to ½" larger than the pattern all around.

3 Using a doubled length of thread, hand sew a basting stitch within the seam allowance, beginning and ending on the right side of the fabric.

Marked line

4 Center the template on the wrong side of the fabric, and pull the thread tightly to gather the fabric around the template. Tie a knot if desired, and press with a hot iron, using steam or starch if needed to create a crisp edge. Remove the template and press the edges once more. If the circle is small, you may need to remove the basting stitches in order to remove the template. Otherwise, you can simply leave them in place.

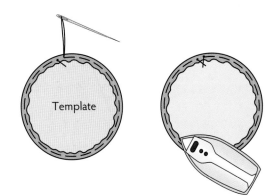

Template

▶ Bias tape is easy to make with a bias tape maker.

▶ Bias tape's inherent stretchiness makes it perfect for creating smooth, flat curves.

BIAS-TAPE APPLIQUÉ

Bias tape, made from fabric that's cut on the bias (diagonal to the grain), is stretchy and pliable, and great for creating curves while still laying flat. To use bias tape for appliqué, simply lay out the bias tape on a base fabric in whatever pattern you wish. Use steam and a hot iron to help stretch the fabric's fibers and manipulate it as needed. Pin or baste the tape in place, and then stitch it by hand or machine.

You can purchase premade bias tape in various sizes and colors, but you can also easily make your own. To make your own bias tape, you need fabric, a bias-tape maker, and a hot iron. Start by cutting your fabric into bias strips—strips cut at a 45° angle to the straight grain or selvage edges of the fabric.

1 Cut bias strips in the width needed for the project and for the bias-tape maker you're using.

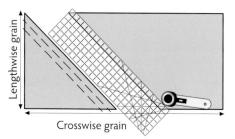

2 If you need a length of tape that's longer than a single bias strip, place strips right sides together at a 90° angle, align the raw edges, offsetting them by ¼" as shown. Sew them together on the diagonal and press the seam allowances open.

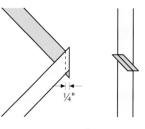

¼"

Press seam open.

3 Feed the strip of bias fabric through the bias-tape maker, and anchor the end of the strip to your ironing surface with a straight pin. Pull the bias tape maker along the length of the strip, following with a hot steam iron to press the folds. Continue to adjust and move the straight pin, anchoring the strip as needed.

A Bit of Appliqué

4 Now you have a length of single-fold bias
  tape, which is folded once on each side
toward the center. To make double-fold bias tape,
fold the tape in half lengthwise and press again
so the raw edges are completely enclosed within
the tape.

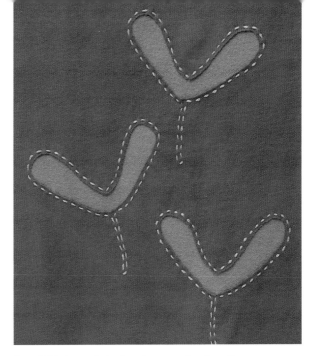

▶ With jersey knit, there's no need to turn the raw
  edges under.

REVERSE APPLIQUÉ

Reverse appliqué involves placing the appliqué
fabric behind the background fabric and cutting
away the top layer of background to reveal the
appliqué fabric below.

1 Attach the appliqué layer to the top layer
  temporarily with pins or by thread basting. The
right side of the appliqué should face the wrong
side of the background.

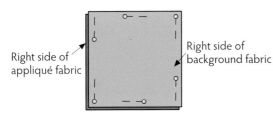

Right side of
appliqué fabric

Right side of
background fabric

2 Mark the shape on the top layer. Carefully
  cut the shape away from the top layer only,
adding a ¼" seam allowance to the inside of
the drawn line. For knits, you can cut directly on
the drawn line. Start by gently pulling the top
layer of fabric away from the appliqué fabric
below, and cutting a small slit in the middle of the
marked shape, then cut toward the marked line.

3 Turn under the seam allowance of the cotton
  fabric and stitch to the bottom layer with
decorative or tiny, almost invisible stitches. With
knit fabrics, stitch the cut edges without turning
them under. After the stitching is complete,
remove pins or basting stitches and cut away the
excess appliqué fabric behind the background.

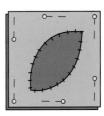

Reverse appliqué can be done with multiple layers
of fabric, revealing two, three, or more prints or
colors below the top one.

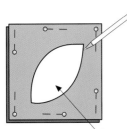

Template

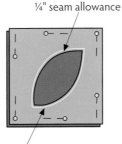

¼" seam allowance

Drawn line

other techniques + tips

In this section you'll find instructions for the hand stitches I use, along with my suggestions and tips for marking fabric, clipping seam allowances, and using interfacing.

HAND STITCHES

I use just a few very basic stitches to make most of my projects. I also include some simple embroidery stitching to add details and embellishment to some of the items.

Appliqué Stitch

I use this for hand appliqué, varying the size of the stitches as a design element. Sometimes I like them to be noticeable and will make them larger. Other times I make them smaller so they're almost invisible and blend in with the appliqué.

Ladder Stitch or Slipstitch

Use this stitch when sewing closed the openings used for turning totes, linings, and stuffed items to the right side.

Running Stitch

The running stitch can be used for actual sewing, or as an embroidery stitch to add details to the design.

Backstitch

This embroidery stitch creates a solid stitching line for embellishing and adding details.

French Knot

The French knot adds texture and can be used for flower centers, eyes, and other design elements.

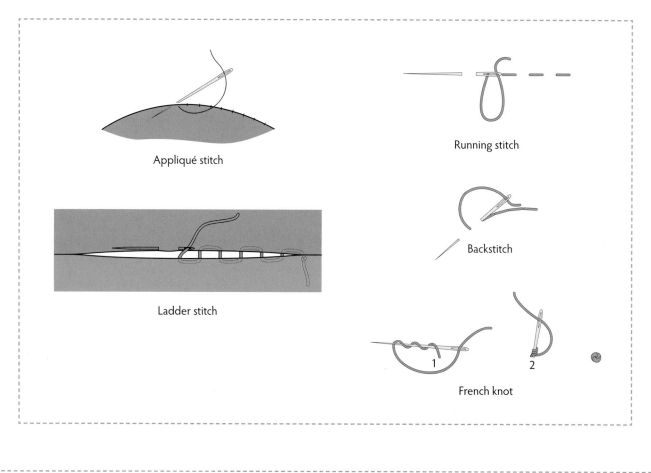

Appliqué stitch

Ladder stitch

Running stitch

Backstitch

French knot

MARKERS AND MARKING

Always test a water-soluble marker first on whatever fabric you're using. My favorite is the Mark-B-Gone by Dritz. I use these pens *a lot* and almost never have a problem removing the marks.

I try to remove the marks before pressing, to make sure that I don't set them with the heat of the iron. To remove, I spritz the marks with water or wipe them off with a damp cloth. Follow the manufacturer's instructions for the particular marker you're using. If the fabric is too wet after removing the marks, press with a dry, hot iron to steam the moisture away.

CLIPPING CURVES AND CORNERS

Clipping or notching curved seams allows them to lie flat and reduces bulk when items are turned to the right side. Be sure that you cut *within the seam allowance only,* and not through the stitches. Notch outside curves and clip inside ones.

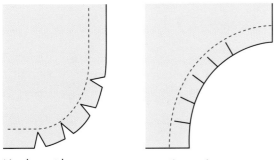

Notch outside curves.   Clip inside curves.

Trimming corners within the seam allowances also reduces bulk and gives the corner a sharper point when turned right side out. Trim corners at a 45° angle just next to the corner of the stitch line.

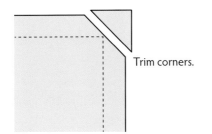

Trim corners.

▶ A cluster of embroidered French knots adds subtle texture to the center of this flower design.

APPLYING FUSIBLE INTERFACING

I strongly recommend following the manufacturer's instructions for each specific type of interfacing used. When I purchase interfacing by the yard, I ask for the thin strip of paper with the fusing instructions as well, and I bundle that up with the interfacing so they always stay together. I also have a few general tips that apply to using any type of fusible interfacing.

Cutting interfacing. Most patterns instruct you to cut interfacing the same size as the fabric it will be fused to. Go ahead and do that. Then trim off an additional ⅛" around all sides, and center it on your fabric before fusing it down to ensure that the interfacing fuses only to your fabric, and not to your ironing surface. Alternately, you can fuse a piece of interfacing larger than your pattern piece to your fabric first, *before* you cut the fabric. This will save a couple of steps, but requires some forethought, and will waste a little more fabric than the first method.

Fusing interfacing. Always check that the fusible side of your interfacing is *facing* the fabric (and not your iron or pressing cloth) before you press it with the iron. Trust me, you do not want to waste a perfectly good pressing cloth, or, even worse, clean that sticky fusible gunk off your iron! If the instructions call for a damp press cloth, dampen one by spritzing it with a water bottle, or by running it under water and wringing it out well.

Sound Waves QUILT

I love the boldness and simplicity of the bias-tape appliqué, curving above and below a single seam on this quilted throw. It makes me think of high and low frequency sound waves on a graph. It's the perfect size to snuggle under in your family room . . . while listening to your favorite tunes.

▶ **FINISHED QUILT:** 55" x 66"

▶ **TECHNIQUE:** Bias-tape appliqué

MATERIALS

Yardage is based on 42"-wide fabric.

1⅔ yards of light-blue cotton print for quilt front*
1⅔ yards of pale-gray cotton print for quilt front*
2¾ yards of ½" single-fold bias tape in a solid color (store-bought or handmade)
1 fat quarter (18" x 21") of solid fabric to make the 6 yards of ⅜" single-fold bias tape**
⅝ yard of cotton fabric for binding
3½ yards of cotton fabric for backing
59" x 70" piece of cotton batting
⅜" bias-tape maker

I used a blue-on-white text print and a white-on-pale gray print.

**If you want to use premade tape, substitute 6 yards of ½"-wide tape.*

CUTTING

From the light-blue print, cut:
1 rectangle, 26½" x 55"

From the pale-gray print, cut:
1 rectangle, 40½" x 55"*

From the fabric for binding, cut:
7 strips, 2¼" x 42"

From the fabric for backing, cut:
2 rectangles, 35½" x 59"

If your fabric isn't quite wide enough to get 40½", it's okay. Just use the width that you have; your quilt will be a bit shorter in length.

MAKING THE QUILT FRONT

Read "Bias-Tape Appliqué" on page 12 before starting project.

1 With right sides together, sew the light-blue and pale-gray print rectangles together along one 55" side using a ½" seam allowance. Press the seam allowances open.

2 Lay out the quilt front, right side up, on a flat surface, or drape over a table so the area at least 12" above and below the seam is flat.

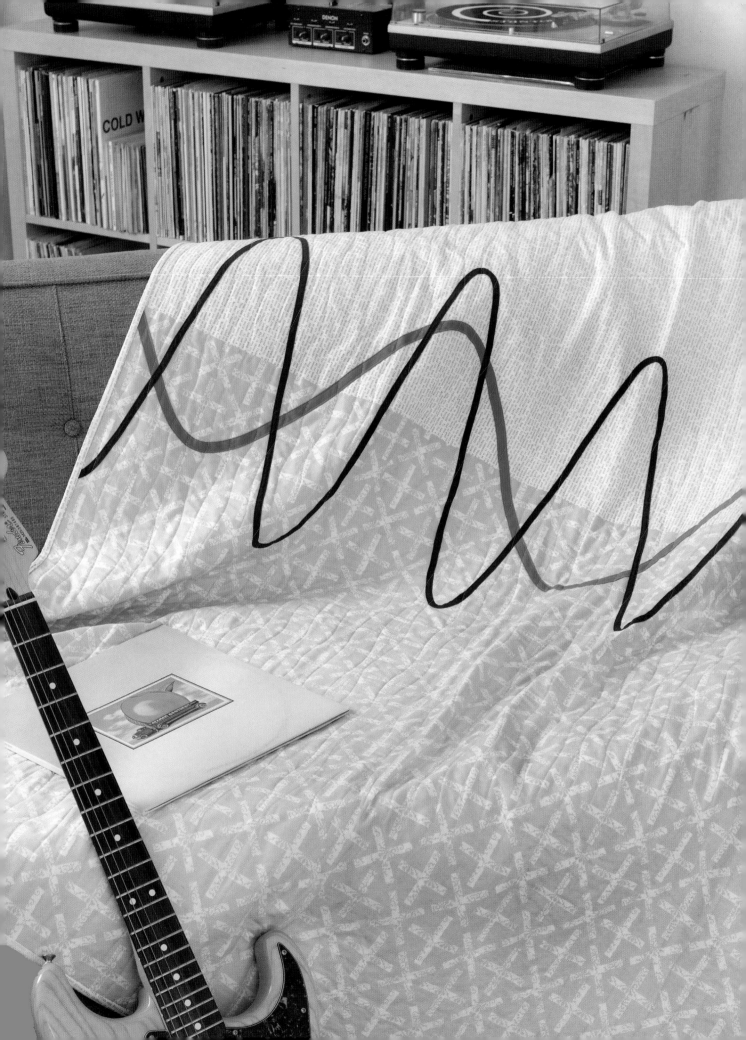

COLD W

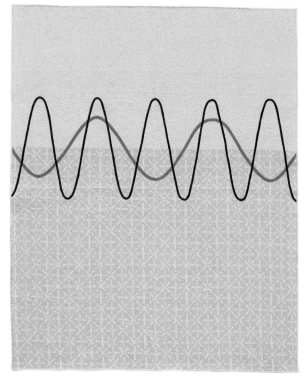

▶ "Sound Waves Quilt"

of steam, press and manipulate the bias tape until you are happy with the curves and the bias tape lies flat. Pin or hand baste to hold the curves in place.

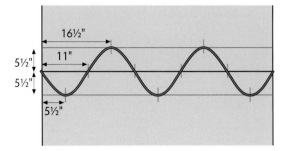

+ Pressing the Curves

If you have a portable pressing board, place it under the quilt top, moving the pressing board (instead of the quilt top) as needed while you press. If not, gently move the quilt top to an ironing board with the bias tape loosely pinned, and then press as needed.

3 For the low wave, mark the quilt front with a water-soluble marker or light-colored chalk every 11" along the seam. At 5½" *above* the seam, make a mark 16½" from the left side, and then 22" from that mark. At 5½" *below* the seam, make a mark 5½" from the left side, and then two more marks 22" apart.

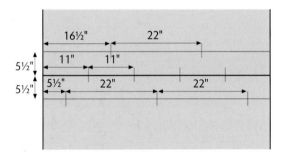

4 Using the marks, create curves with the ½"-wide bias tape. The curves should cross the seam at the 11" marks, and the "hills" and "valleys" should touch the marks 5½" above and below the seam. Use pins to temporarily hold the bias tape in place. With a hot iron and plenty

5 Edgestitch along both sides of the bias tape to complete the appliqué. Remove any basting stitches.

6 For the high wave, mark the quilt front with a water-soluble marker or light-colored chalk. Along the seam line, mark 2¾" from the left edge, and then every 5½". At 9" *above* the seam line, mark 5½" from the left edge, and then every 11". At 9" *below* the seam line, mark every 11".

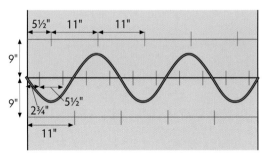

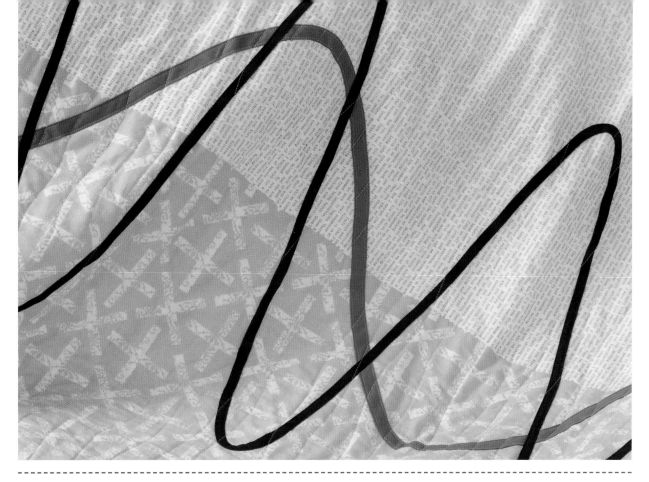

▶ Two colors and widths of bias tape are the focus of this quilt. Narrower tape is used for the tighter curves; wider tape for the gentler curves.

7 Using the marks, create curves with the ⅜"-wide bias tape. Use pins to temporarily hold the bias tape in place. With a hot iron and plenty of steam, press and manipulate the bias tape until you are happy with the curves and the bias tape lies flat. Pin or hand baste to hold the curves in place.

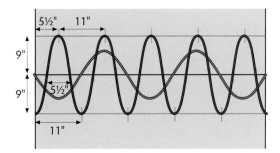

8 Edgestitch along both sides of the bias tape to complete the appliqué. Remove any basting stitches.

FINISHING THE QUILT

1 With right sides together, sew the two backing pieces together along one 59" side using a ½" seam allowance. Press the seam allowances open.

2 Make a quilt sandwich by layering the batting on top of the backing, right side down, and then centering the quilt top on the batting, right side up. Pin or thread baste the layers together.

3 Quilt as desired. Then trim excess batting and backing even with the quilt top.

4 Prepare and sew the binding to the quilt. If you're unfamiliar with how to make and attach binding, see ShopMartingale.com/HowtoQuilt for free illustrated information.

Retro Flower TOTE

Perfect for a picnic or a day at the beach, this roomy tote is embellished with a charming oversized daisy. Each petal shows off a different print, and a scattering of French knots at the flower's center adds extra elegance. The gentle curves of the petals are ideal for turned edge appliqué, making this bag as durable as it is lovely.

▶ **FINISHED TOTE:** 11" x 18½" x 5"
▶ **TECHNIQUES:** Turned-edge appliqué with freezer paper, gathered-circle appliqué, and embroidery

MATERIALS

Yardage is based on 42"-wide fabric.

1⅛ yards of cotton print for tote lining
¾ yard of linen/cotton blend fabric for tote
⅓ yard or 1 fat quarter (18" x 21") *each* of 5 different cotton prints for flower appliqué
¼ yard of dark solid canvas for tote bottom
¼ yard of cotton print for handle lining
5" square of light-blue cotton solid for flower center
1½ yards of 20"-wide woven lightweight fusible interfacing (such as Pellon's Shape-Flex)
¾ yard of 18"-wide fusible web
Embroidery floss in light blue

CUTTING

From the linen/cotton blend fabric, cut:
2 squares, 17" x 17"
2 strips, 2½" x 21"

From the print for tote lining, cut:
2 rectangles, 17" x 22"
2 rectangles, 13" x 14"

From the canvas, cut:
2 rectangles, 6" x 17"

From the print for handle lining, cut:
2 strips, 2½" x 21"

From the interfacing, cut:
2 squares, 16½" x 16½"
1 rectangle, 12½" x 13½"
2 strips, 2" x 20½"

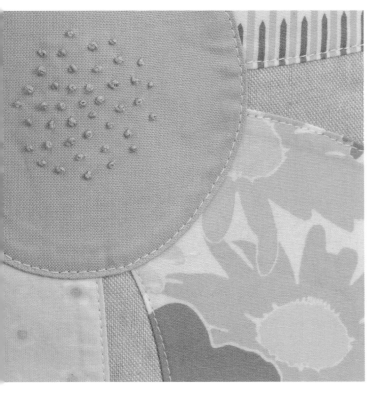

▶ A simple straight stitch is all you need to secure the turned-edge appliqué.

EMBELLISHING THE TOTE

1 Center the 16½" square of interfacing on the wrong side of a linen/cotton blend 17" square for the tote front panel and fuse, following the manufacturer's instructions. Repeat with the tote back panel.

2 Trace the flower-petal patterns onto freezer paper and cut out.

3 Following the instructions in "Turned-Edge Appliqué with Freezer Paper" on page 10, iron a freezer-paper template for petal A onto the wrong side of one the prints for the flower petals. Cut the fabric, adding seam allowances to the long curved edges as indicated on the pattern. Press the seam allowances toward the freezer paper, peel off the paper, and then press the fabric again. Repeat for petals B, C, D, and E.

4 Trace the flower-petal patterns onto the paper side of fusible web, and cut out slightly *inside* the traced lines, so each shape is a bit smaller than the pattern. Following the manufacturer's instructions, iron the fusible web to the wrong side of each prepared petal shape. Remove the paper backing.

5 Using the "Turned-Edge Appliqué with Freezer Paper" method or "Gathered-Circle Appliqué" method on page 11, create a turned-edge circle from the light-blue fabric using the pattern for the flower center on page 25.

6 Trace the circle pattern onto the paper side of fusible web, and cut out slightly *inside* the traced lines, so the shape is a bit smaller than the pattern. Following the manufacturer's instructions, iron the fusible web to the wrong side of the circle. Remove the paper backing.

7 Lay the flower petals on the right side of the tote front panel. You may want to do this directly on your ironing surface, so you don't need to worry about moving the panel after the appliqué shapes are in place. Align the raw edges and use the illustration as a guide for placement. Add the circle to the center of the flower. It should overlap the raw edges of the flower petals at the center by about ¼". Adjust the flower petals as needed. Following the manufacturer's instructions, fuse all the pieces to the tote front.

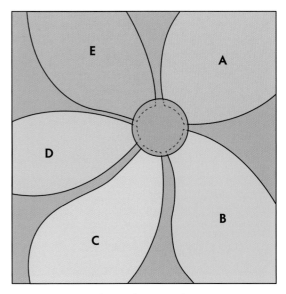

Appliqué placement diagram

A Bit of Appliqué

8 Using a straight stitch and a neutral thread color, topstitch around the edges of the appliqués.

9 Using three strands of embroidery floss, stitch French knots in the center of the circle.

MAKING THE TOTE

All seam allowances are ½".

1 With right sides together and raw edges aligned, pin and sew the long edge of one canvas 6" x 17" tote bottom to the bottom of the front panel. Repeat with the other tote bottom and the back panel. Press the seam allowances toward the tote bottom.

2 Using thread to match the canvas, topstitch ⅛" below the seam.

3 Place the front and back panels right sides together, matching raw edges. Pin the panels in place, and then stitch along the sides and bottom edge, leaving the top open. Press the seam allowances open.

4 To create the gusset for the tote bottom, fold the sides at one bottom corner so that the side seam is aligned with the bottom seam. Use a fabric-marking pen to draw a line perpendicular to the side seam, 2½" from the point. The line will be 5" long. Stitch along this line, and then stitch again ⅛" inside the previous stitching to reinforce the gusset. Trim the seam allowances to ½". Repeat with the second bottom corner. Turn the tote right side out and set aside.

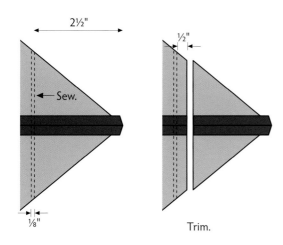

MAKING THE LINING AND POCKET

1 Center the 12½" x 13½" rectangle of interfacing on one print 13" x 14" pocket piece and fuse, following the manufacturer's instructions. Place pocket pieces right sides together and pin. Sew along the raw edges, leaving a 3" opening along one 14" side for turning.

2 Trim corners and turn the pocket right side out. Use a point turner, knitting needle, or similar tool to gently push out corners. Press the seam allowances under ½" along the opening.

3 Topstitch ⅛" to ¼" from the top edge of the pocket (the edge opposite the one with the opening).

4 Place the pocket on the right side of one print 17" x 22" lining piece; center it 4½" below one of the 17" edges as shown. Pin the pocket in place and sew it to the lining along the sides and bottom, close to the edge.

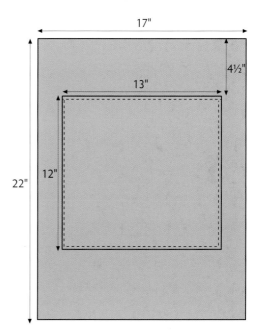

5 Place the lining panels right sides together, with raw edges aligned. Pin the panels in place and stitch along the sides and bottom, leaving the top open. Press the seam allowances open.

6 To create the gusset, follow step 4 of "Making the Tote" on page 23. Leave the lining inside out and set aside.

MAKING THE HANDLES

1 Center the interfacing strips on the wrong side of the linen/cotton 2½" x 21" strips and fuse, following the manufacturer's instructions.

2 Pin one handle to one handle lining, keeping right sides together and raw edges aligned. Sew along one long edge only. Repeat with the second handle and handle lining. Turn the handles right side out and press the sewn edge.

3 Along the long raw edge of each handle and handle lining, fold ½" to the wrong side and press. With wrong sides together and folded edges aligned, topstitch ⅛" from the folded edges of each handle.

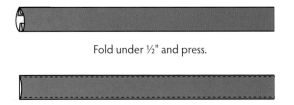

Fold under ½" and press.

Topstitch.

+ Another Option

You can also sew the handles together along both long sides to make a tube. Then turn the tube right side out. Press and topstitch ⅛" from the edges.

FINISHING THE TOTE

1 Pin one handle to the tote front, with the raw edges aligned and the centers of the handle strip 4½" in from the side seam as shown. The lining of the handle should be facing out. Repeat with the second handle on the tote back. Baste the handles ¼" from the raw edges of the tote front and back.

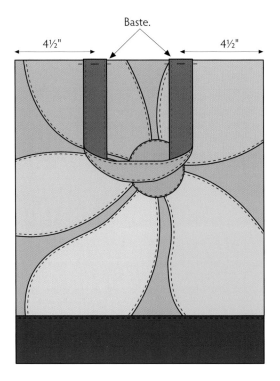

Baste.

4½"   4½"

2 Carefully place the tote inside the lining, so right sides are together and handles are tucked inside. Align the side seams and pin. Stitch around the raw edge, leaving a 6" opening between the handles along the back of the tote.

3 Turn the tote right side out through the opening. Press the top edge, turning under the seam allowances along the opening. Pin the opening closed, and then topstitch along the entire top edge of the tote.

+ Make a Throw Pillow

To make a throw pillow from this pattern, cut one linen/cotton 17" square for the pillow front—add interfacing if desired—and two cotton 12½" x 17" rectangles for the back panels. First, follow the instructions for "Embellishing the Tote" on page 22 to create the pillow front. To finish the pillow, follow instructions for "Assembling the Pillow" on page 45 of "Prairie Blooms Throw Pillow" to hem the 17" sides of the back panels, and then sew the back panels to the front.

▶ A fabulous throw pillow is perfect for dressing up your sofa or adding color to a chair.

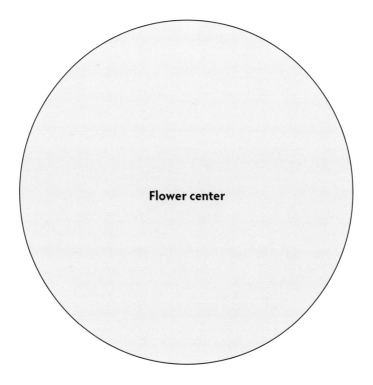

Flower center

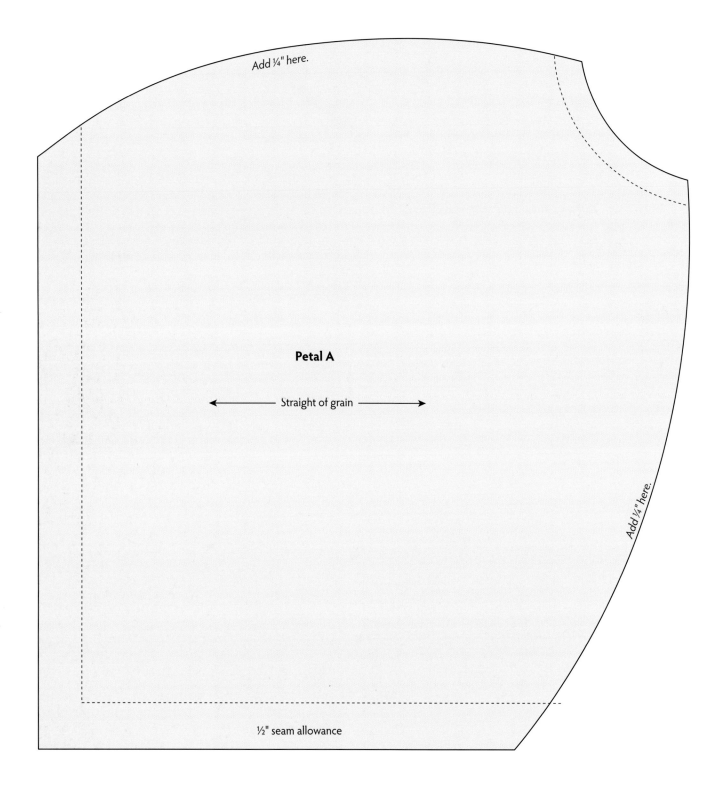

Add ¼" here.

Petal A

⟵ Straight of grain ⟶

Add ¼" here.

½" seam allowance

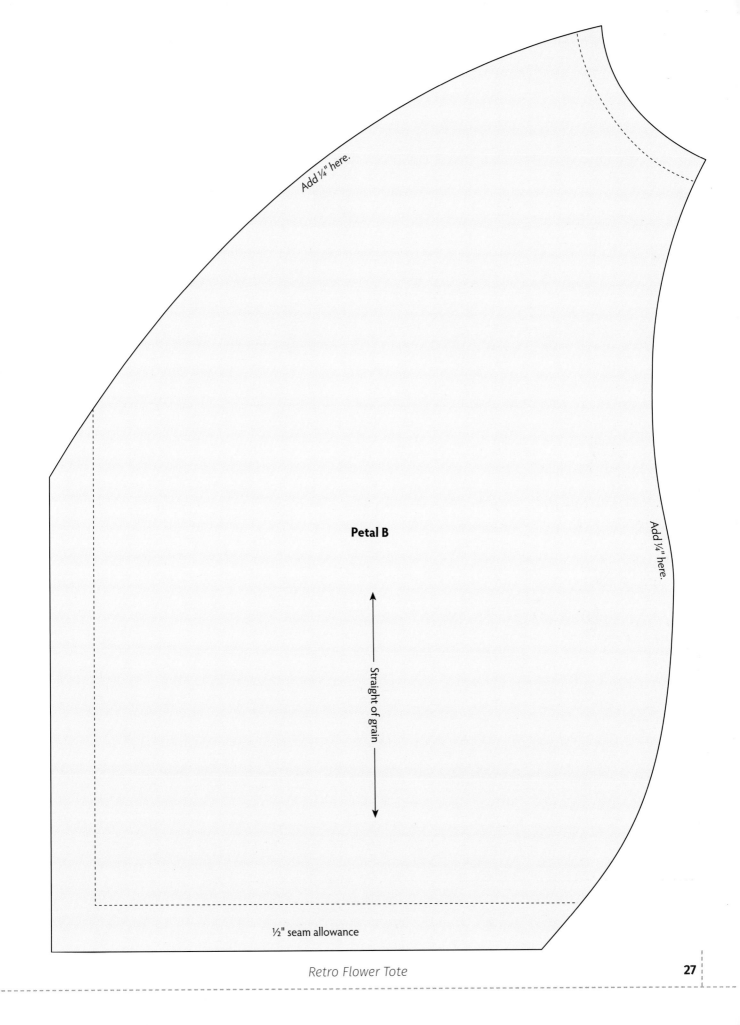

Add ¼" here.

Petal B

Add ¼" here.

Straight of grain

½" seam allowance

Retro Flower Tote

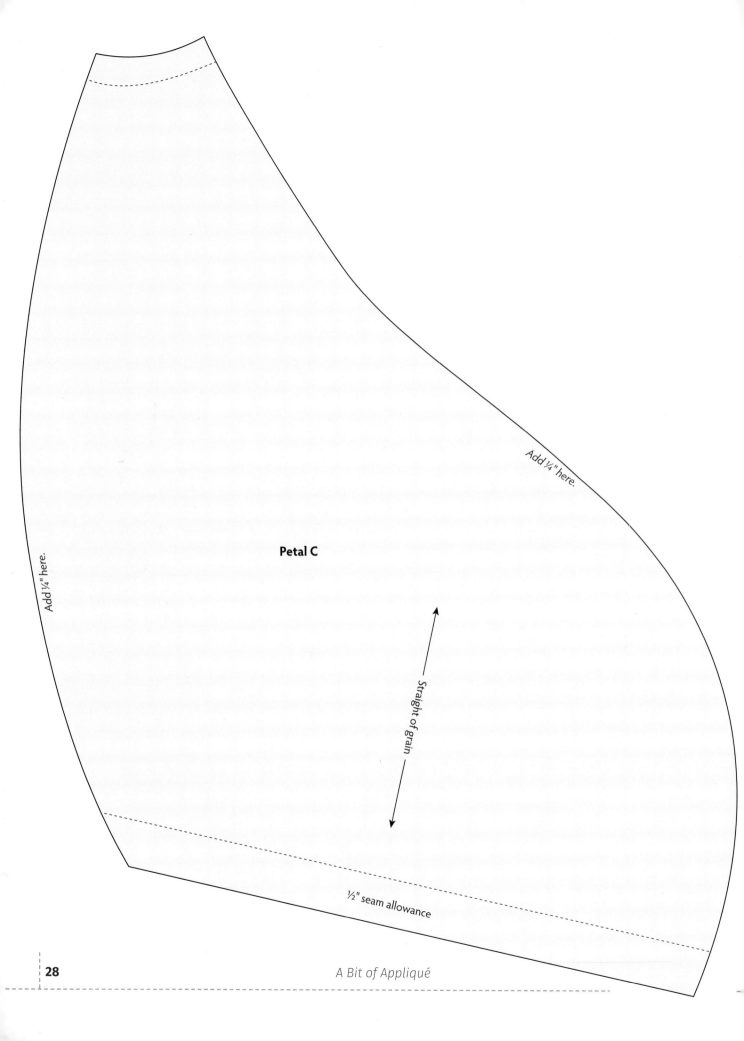

Petal C

Add ¼" here.

Add ¼" here.

Straight of grain

½" seam allowance

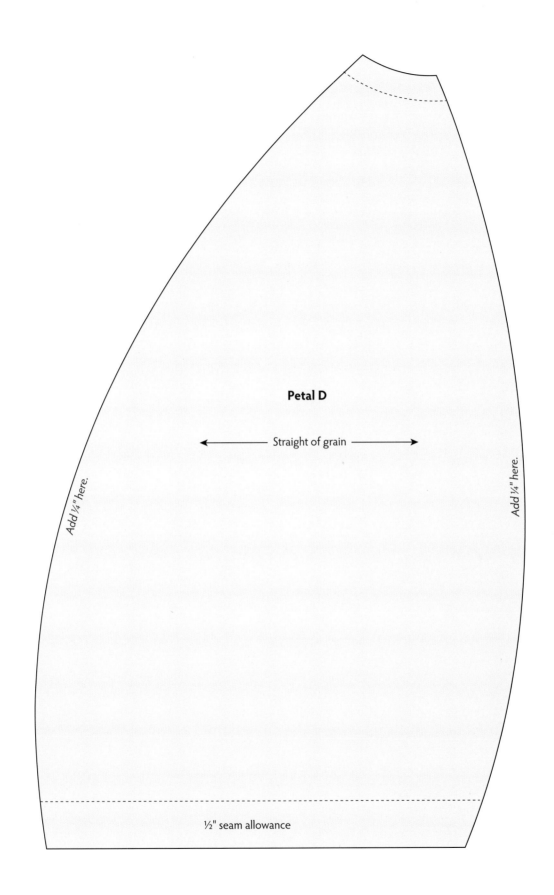

Petal D

← Straight of grain →

Add ¼" here.

Add ¼" here.

½" seam allowance

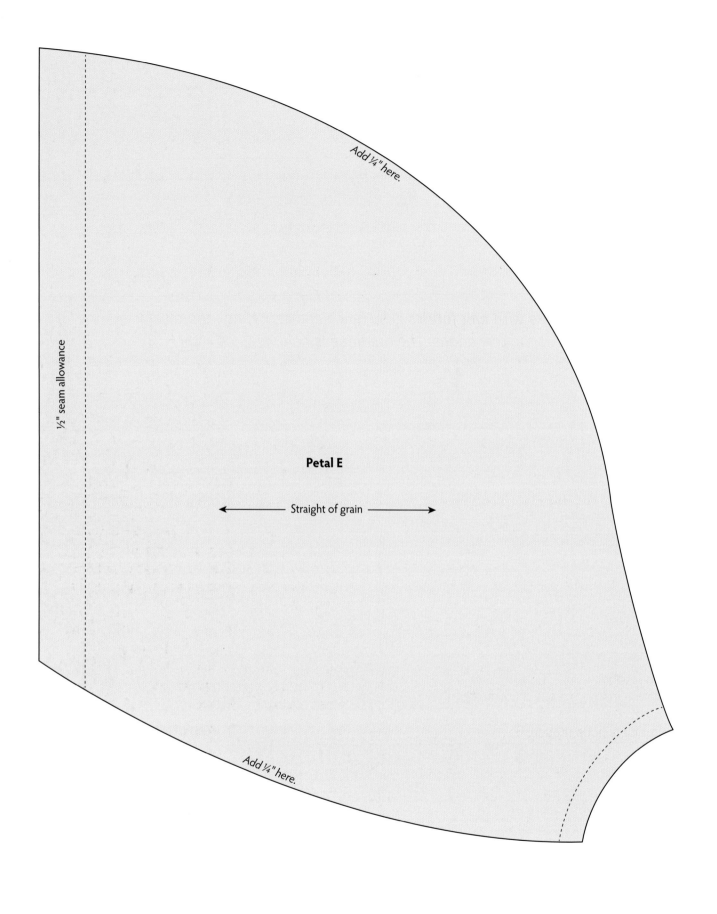

Add ¼" here.

½" seam allowance

Petal E

← Straight of grain →

Add ¼" here.

Seedpod T-SHIRT

This design pays homage to the wondrous, twirling maple tree seedpod, also known as a "whirligig" or "helicopter" seed. The reverse-appliqué technique used here with knit fabrics is so quick and satisfying—there's no need to turn under the raw edges. The appliqué is held in place with contrasting pearl-cotton thread.

▶ **FINISHED SIZE:** T-shirt shown, woman's small

▶ **TECHNIQUES:** Reverse appliqué and embroidery

MATERIALS

Cotton jersey T-shirt in dark gray
12" square of cotton jersey fabric in violet*
Pearl-cotton thread, size 5, in teal
Ballpoint embroidery needle
Freezer paper
Water-soluble marker or chalk marker in light color
Embroidery hoop (optional)

*I cut this from a second, thrifted T-shirt.

EMBELLISHING THE T-SHIRT

1 Using the pattern on page 33, trace three seedpod shapes onto freezer paper and cut out on the drawn lines.

2 Arrange the shapes on the right side of the T-shirt, near the bottom-right corner, as shown in the photo. Make sure they all fit within an 11" square area. Iron the freezer-paper shapes to the shirt.

3 Trace around each shape with a water-soluble marker. Draw a second line around each shape that is about ⅛" outside of the first line, and then add a stem that is about 1½" to 2" long, ⅛" wide, and slightly curved.

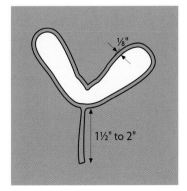

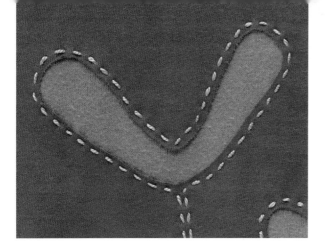

4 Place the square of violet fabric against the wrong side of the T-shirt, so it is tucked inside the shirt and is positioned behind the seedpod shapes. Smooth the violet fabric out, being careful not to stretch it, and baste in place around the outer edges using a ballpoint needle and sewing thread.

+ Pinning vs. Basting

If you'd rather pin the background fabric in place with safety pins or straight pins, work slowly and carefully. Be sure that the sharp points of the pins don't damage the knit fabric by piercing through the fibers, but rather slip in between the knitted threads of the fabric. If you encounter resistance with the pins, simply pull them back and try a different spot.

5 Peel off the freezer-paper shapes.

6 Using a ballpoint needle and pearl-cotton thread, embroider each seedpod with a running stitch. Follow the outermost lines and the stems that you drew in step 3. Referring to "Securing the Embroidery Stitches" above right, secure the thread at the beginning and end of each shape, and begin embroidering each seedpod with a new length of thread. I find it easiest to manipulate the fabric without an embroidery hoop, but you might prefer to use one. Do whatever feels most comfortable for you.

+ Securing the Embroidery Stitches

To reduce bulk on the inside of the T-shirt, I don't tie a knot when I begin embroidering. Instead, I pull the thread through, leaving a tail about 3" to 4" long on the wrong side of the fabric. When I've completed embroidering around the shape, I tie the starting and ending tails together to secure. Then I thread each tail under a couple of the adjacent stitches before I trim them.

7 To complete the reverse appliqué and reveal the colored fabric behind, gently pull the violet fabric away from the T-shirt fabric and cut a small slit in the T-shirt fabric with small, sharp scissors. Then carefully cut all the way around the marked inner line of the seedpod, without cutting into the violet fabric.

8 Remove the basting stitches, turn the T-shirt inside out, and trim the excess violet fabric about ¼" from the embroidered stitching.

9 Turn the T-shirt right side out again and use an iron with steam to "repair" or close up any holes that might remain in the fabric from the basting stitches or pins.

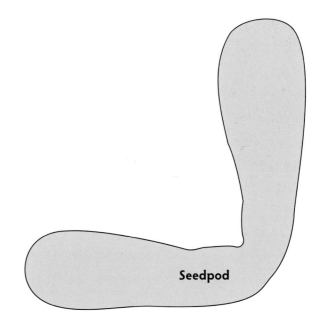

Seedpod

Sunny Day PATCH

Inspired by a paper collage my son made in art class, this felt patch is made with scraps of sunny orange and yellow fabrics. I used it to adorn the back of a child's jean jacket. This quick and cheerful project is a great way to make use of all those little scraps of fabric you've been saving!

▶ **FINISHED PATCH:** Approximately 6½" x 6½"
▶ **TECHNIQUES:** Raw-edge felt appliqué and raw-edge fusible appliqué

MATERIALS

7½" x 7½" square of yellow wool felt for backing
5" x 5" square of yellow cotton solid for sun
Scraps of assorted orange and yellow cotton fabrics, 2" x 2", for sunrays
⅜ yard of 18"-wide fusible web
All-purpose sewing thread in yellow
Yellow embroidery floss (optional)

MAKING THE SUN APPLIQUÉ

1 Referring to "Raw-Edge Fusible Appliqué" on page 8 and using the patterns on page 37, trace 20 triangle shapes (5 of each shape) and one circle onto the paper side of the fusible web. Roughly cut around each shape. Fuse the triangles to the wrong side of the orange and yellow fabric scraps, and the circle to the wrong side of the yellow 5" square. Cut out the shapes on the drawn lines.

2 With the paper backing still attached, place the circle fabric side down in the center of the felt square and trace around it with chalk or a dull pencil. Set the yellow circle aside.

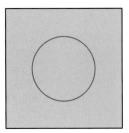

▶ Use an assortment of fabric scraps for the triangular sun rays.

+ **Arranging the Appliqué Pieces**

Work directly on your ironing surface when positioning the appliqué pieces onto the felt. You don't want to arrange all the tiny pieces and then have them shift as you move them to your ironing board.

3 Peel away the paper backing of the triangular pieces and arrange them around the drawn circle on the felt as shown. Place the triangles down one at a time, so the base of each triangle extends about ¼" inside the circle and the bottom corner of each successive triangle overlaps the preceding one. Alternate the shapes and fabrics. When you complete the circle, you'll probably have several triangles left over. Save them for another project or discard them.

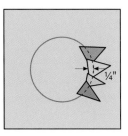

4 Fuse the triangles to the felt, following the manufacturer's instructions.

5 Peel away the paper backing of the circle and place it in the center of the triangles so it overlaps all of the triangle bases. Fuse the circle in place, following the manufacturer's instructions.

6 Using yellow thread and a straight stitch, machine stitch the appliqué pieces in place.

+ Stitching the Appliqués

To maneuver the curves of the center appliqué shape, stitch slowly. You may also need to stop often, with your needle in the down position. Then raise the presser foot and pivot. For inside and outside points, stop with the needle down, raise the presser foot, pivot, and continue stitching down the opposite edge of the appliqué piece.

FINISHING THE PATCH

1 If you wish to fuse the patch in place before sewing it to the garment or other item, center a 7" square of fusible web on the wrong side of the felt square. Press to adhere the fusible web, following the manufacturer's instructions

2 Trim the felt around the triangular sunrays, leaving a border of about ⅛". Trim the pointed ends of the felt flat, as shown in the photo on page 36.

3 Fuse or pin the sun to the desired surface and hand or machine stitch in place. I stitched by hand using three strands of yellow embroidery floss and a running stitch to attach the patch to the back of a jean jacket.

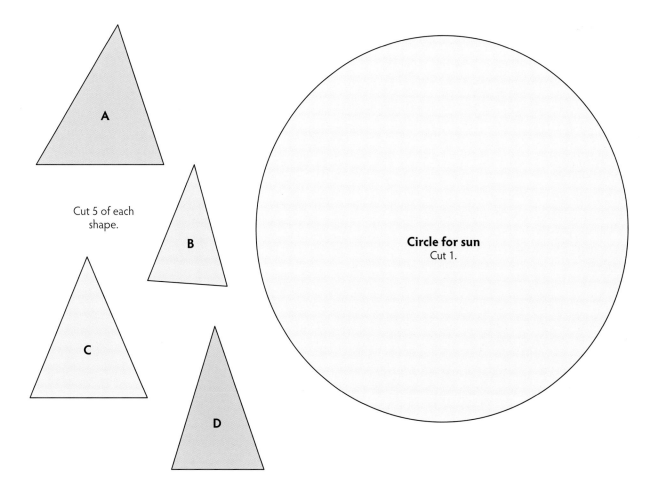

A

Cut 5 of each shape.

B

C

D

Circle for sun
Cut 1.

Garden SKIRT

*A **sketch of a flower garden my daughter drew for me** inspired the motifs on this simple skirt for girls' sizes 4 through 12. I loved her unique take on the flowers' petals and leaves—and how happy the drawing looked! To accentuate the playful feel of the original drawing, the raw-edge appliqué is held in place and embellished with colorful embroidery floss.*

▶ **FINISHED SKIRT:** Girls' sizes 4 to 12

▶ **TECHNIQUES:** Raw-edge fusible appliqué, bias-tape appliqué, and embroidery

MATERIALS

Yardage is based on 42"-wide fabric.

⅞ yard of blue cotton chambray for sizes up to 10 OR 1⅓ yards for size 12

⅔ yard of green ¼"-wide single-fold bias tape or grosgrain ribbon for stems

Scraps of 2 light-green cotton fabrics, at least 3" x 3", for leaves

Scraps of 4 colorful cotton fabrics, at least 3" x 3", for flowers

Embroidery floss in coordinating colors

¼ yard of 18"-wide fusible web

1 yard of 1"-wide braided, knit, or non-roll elastic

CUTTING

Using the chart on page 40, choose the skirt size based on waist and height measurements.

From the chambray fabric, cut:
2 fabric panels as indicated in the chart

▶ My daughter's whimsical drawing inspired a colorful appliqué design.

Skirt Sizes, Finished Length, and Cutting Dimensions							
Size	4	5	6	7	8	10	12
Waist	21½"	22"	22½"	23"	23½"	24½"	25½"
Height	39"–42"	42"–45"	45"–48"	48"–51"	51"–54"	54"–58"	58"–60"
Skirt length	12½"	13½"	14½"	15½"	16½"	17½"	18½"
Fabric panels	21½" x 15"	22" x 16"	22½" x 17"	23" x 18"	23½" x 19"	24½" x 20"	25½" x 21"
Elastic	22½"	23"	23½"	24"	24½"	25½"	26½"

PREPARING THE APPLIQUÉS

1 Referring to "Raw-Edge Fusible Appliqué" on page 8, trace the patterns for flower and leaf shapes from page 41 onto the paper side of the fusible web, leaving at least ½" of space between each shape. Cut out each shape, leaving roughly a ¼" border. Following the manufacturer's instructions, fuse the shapes to the wrong side of the fabrics. Allow the fabric to cool, and then cut along the traced lines and remove the paper backing.

2 Cut the bias tape or ribbon into three 8" lengths.

EMBELLISHING THE SKIRT

1 Lay one chambray panel right side up, with the long edges at the top and bottom. Position the appliqué shapes and stems on the fabric as shown in the placement guide at right so that the stem on the right is approximately 3" from the edge. The stems should overlap the leaves, and the flowers should overlap the stems, by at least ⅛". The stems should also extend past the bottom raw edge of the chambray panel. Pin the shapes in place.

2 Following the manufacturer's instructions, fuse only the leaves in place, removing and replacing the pins and stems as necessary. You can also leave the stems in place and iron right over them.

3 With matching thread, topstitch near the long edges of each stem, folding the flower shapes out of the way as needed. Trim the bottom ends of the stems even with the raw edge of the fabric.

4 Remove the remaining pins and fuse the flowers in place.

5 Using three strands of embroidery floss and an appliqué stitch, sew around all of the fused leaf and flower shapes. Again, using three strands of embroidery floss, embroider the leaves on flower A with a backstitch. Use a backstitch and French knots to embellish flower B as shown.

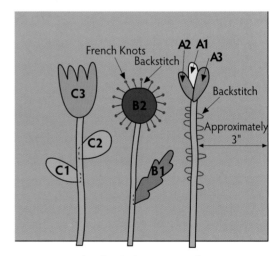

Appliqué placement guide

FINISHING THE SKIRT

1 To sew the skirt panels together with nicely finished French seams, place the panels wrong sides together and sew each short side using a ¼" seam allowance. Trim the seam allowances to ⅛" and press them to one side. Turn the panels so that right sides are together and sew each seam again using a ¼" seam allowance, encasing the first seam inside. Press the seam allowances toward the back, and then turn the skirt right side out.

2 Turn the bottom edge of the skirt under ¼" and press. Turn the edge under another ⅜", press again, and pin. Topstitch on the right side of the skirt, ¼" from the folded edge.

3 Turn the top edge of the skirt under ½" and press. Turn the edge under another 1½" to make a casing, press again, and pin. Topstitch from the right side of the skirt, 1¼" from the folded edge, leaving a 3" opening at the back for feeding the elastic through.

4 Cut the elastic to the length indicated on the chart. Feed the elastic through the casing, overlap the ends by 1", and pin. Sew the elastic ends together securely, tuck them into the waistband, and then sew the opening closed. Adjust the fabric around the elastic so the gathers are even all the way around.

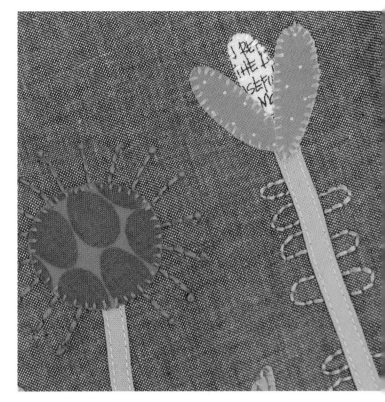

▶ Embroidered details enhance the playful feel of these flowers.

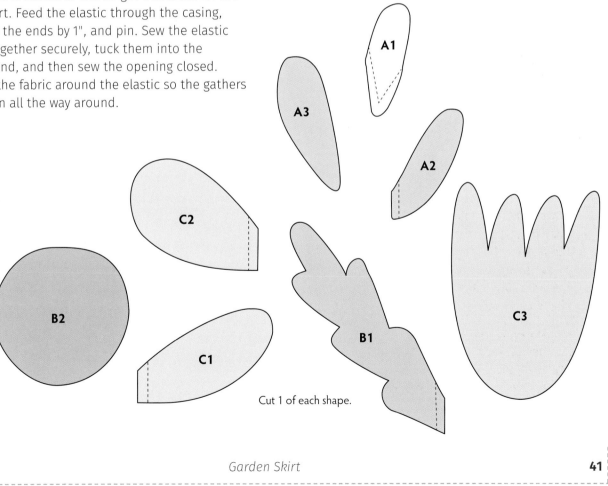

A1

A3

A2

C2

B2

C1

B1

C3

Cut 1 of each shape.

Prairie Blooms THROW PILLOW

Inspired by the tall prairie plants of the Midwest, this throw pillow features wool-felt "blooms" on beautiful natural-colored linen/cotton blend fabric. The stems look hand-sketched, but are quickly stitched by machine.

▶ **FINISHED PILLOW:** 12" x 22"
▶ **TECHNIQUE:** Raw-edge felt appliqué

MATERIALS

Yardage is based on 42"-wide fabric.

½ yard of natural linen/cotton blend fabric for pillow front
½ yard of cotton print for pillow back
Scraps of 4 colors of wool felt, approximately 4" x 4", for appliqué blooms*
¾ yard of 20"-wide woven lightweight fusible interfacing (such as Pellon's Shape-Flex)
¼ yard of 18"-wide fusible web
Water-soluble marker
Medium-green all-purpose thread (or top-stitching thread)
All-purpose thread in colors to match felt
12" x 22" pillow form

I used gold, cranberry, sage, and rust wool felt.

CUTTING

From the linen/cotton blend fabric, cut:
1 rectangle, 13" x 23"

From the cotton print, cut:
2 rectangles, 13" x 15"

From the interfacing, cut:
1 rectangle, 12½" x 22½"

CUTTING THE APPLIQUÉS

Make cardstock templates for patterns A and B on page 45. Trace the templates onto the paper side of fusible web. Roughly cut around each shape, fuse to the felt as indicated below, and cut out the blooms on the drawn lines.

From the gold felt, cut:
2 of bloom A
1 of bloom B

From the cranberry felt, cut:
1 of bloom A
2 of bloom B

From the rust felt, cut:
1 of bloom A
2 of bloom B

From the sage felt, cut:
1 of bloom A
1 of bloom B

EMBELLISHING THE PILLOW FRONT

1 Referring to "Applying Fusible Interfacing" on page 15, center and fuse the interfacing to the wrong side of the linen/cotton pillow front.

2 Arrange the felt blooms on the right side of the pillow front, as shown in the diagram.

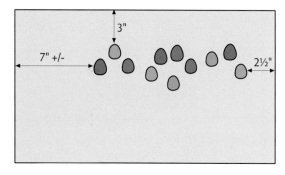

Bloom placement guide

3 When you are happy with the arrangement, use a water-soluble marker to draw stems from the blooms to the bottom edge of the pillow front. Rearrange the angles of the blooms as you do this until you are again happy with the arrangement. Then remove the paper from the blooms and pin each bloom in place to temporarily secure them.

4 Using the medium-green thread and a longer-than-normal stitch length, stitch two or three times along each stem that you drew. When you reach the felt blooms, fold them up a bit so you can extend your stitches ¼" or so beneath them.

+ Stitching the Stems

Don't worry about perfection—this pillow should look as though you're sketching or painting with your sewing machine. Allow the lines of stitching to cross over each other and don't follow the drawn lines too precisely. Be loose and have fun with this! If you prefer, stitch each stem using a narrow satin stitch or hand embroidery.

5 Remove the marks for the stems, referring to "Markers and Marking" on page 15.

6 Fuse the felt blooms in place, following the manufacturer's instructions. You may need to tack each one in place with the tip of a hot iron as you remove the pins, and before fully fusing them, to keep them from shifting or moving out of place.

7 Using matching thread, machine stitch each appliqué to the pillow front. I used a straight stitch about 1⁄16" from the edge of the felt.

+ Securing the Appliqué Stitches

Rather than backstitching when machine sewing around the appliqués, I prefer to pull the thread through to the wrong side of the fabric and tie a knot. That way, I can be absolutely sure the stitches are secure.

ASSEMBLING THE PILLOW

1 Fold and press ½" to the wrong side along one 13" edge of a print 13" x 15" back panel. Fold and press an additional ½" to the wrong side along the same edge. Pin the hem in place. Repeat with the second back panel.

2 Using matching thread, sew the hems by topstitching ⅜" from the folded edges on the right sides of both panels.

3 Lay the pillow front on a flat surface with the right side up. Lay the back panels on the pillow front with the right sides down and all raw edges aligned. The hemmed edges of the back panels will overlap by about 5" at the center. Pin the panels in place. Using a ½" seam allowance, sew around all edges of the pillow cover.

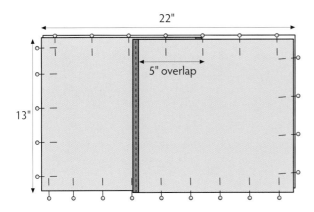

4 Trim the corners diagonally to reduce bulk. Turn the pillow cover right side out, gently pushing the corners out with a point turner, knitting needle, or similar tool. Press the pillow cover and insert the pillow form through the overlapped edges on the pillow back.

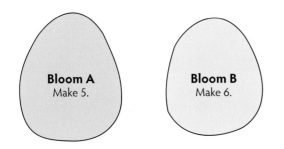

Bloom A
Make 5.

Bloom B
Make 6.

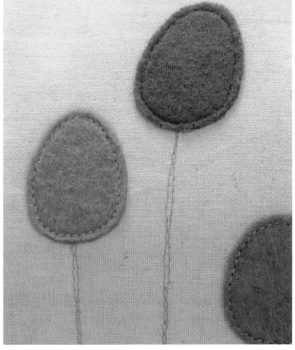

▶ The imperfect "sketched" stems add to the charm of this pillow and complement the natural look of the linen background.

Petals POT HOLDER AND TRIVET

The rich hues and texture of solid linen fabrics are given center stage
in a quilted pot holder and trivet set. The technique is reverse appliqué
with clean, turned edges, and it works so well with the gentle curves of this
geometric petal shape. Try it with solids for the petal shapes, as shown, or
mix it up to highlight your favorite print fabrics against a solid background.

▶ **FINISHED POT HOLDER:** 9½" x 9½"
▶ **FINISHED TRIVET:** 12½" x 15½"
▶ **TECHNIQUE:** Reverse appliqué

MATERIALS FOR 1 POT HOLDER AND 1 TRIVET

Yardage is based on 42"-wide fabric.

½ yard of black-and-white cotton print for
    backgrounds
½ yard of the same or coordinating cotton fabric
    for backing
¼ yard or 1 fat quarter (18" x 21") *each* of 4 cotton
    or linen/cotton blend solids for appliqué*
3 yards of ½"-wide double-fold bias tape (store-
    bought or handmade)
11" x 11" square of low-loft cotton batting for
    pot holder

*I used linen blends in chartreuse, tangerine,
teal, and red.

15" x 18" piece of low-loft cotton batting for trivet
11" x 11" square of insulated batting (such as
    Insul-Bright) for pot holder
15" x 18" piece of insulated batting for trivet
Thin, sharp hand-sewing needle for appliqué
Thread to match background fabric and bias tape
Chalk and water-soluble marker

CUTTING FOR POT HOLDER

From the black-and-white print, cut:
4 squares, 5" x 5"

From *each* of the solids, cut:
1 square, 5" x 5" (4 total)

From the fabric for backing, cut:
1 square, 11" x 11"

Continued on page 48

Continued from page 46

CUTTING FOR TRIVET

From the black-and-white print, cut:
4 squares, 5" x 5"
7 squares, 3½" x 3½"
1 square, 6½" x 6½"

From the chartreuse solid, cut:
3 squares, 5" x 5"
1 square, 3½" x 3½"

From the tangerine solid, cut:
1 square, 5" x 5"
2 squares, 3½" x 3½"

From the teal solid, cut:
4 squares, 3½" x 3½"

From the red solid, cut:
1 square, 6½" x 6½"

From the fabric for backing, cut:
1 rectangle, 15" x 18"

ASSEMBLING THE POT-HOLDER BLOCKS

All seam allowances are ¼".

1. Place one black-and-white 5" square on top of one solid 5" square, both right side up. Machine baste ⅛" from the raw edges around all four sides. Repeat with the remaining three black-and-white and solid 5" squares.

2. Make a cardstock or paper template for the medium petal using the pattern on page 51.

3. With the black-and-white side of a basted square facing up, place the medium-petal template on top, centering it on the diagonal as shown.

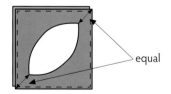
equal

4. Trace around the template with chalk or a water-soluble marker. Remove the template and mark a dashed line ¼" inside the solid lines you traced. This will be your cutting line.

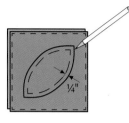
¼"

+ Have a Steady Hand?

If you feel confident cutting without drawing a cutting line first, you can save time by skipping the dashed line in step 4.

---

5. Carefully pinch just the top layer of black-and-white fabric in the center of the drawn shape. Cut a short slit with small, sharp scissors in the top layer of fabric only. Using this slit as a starting point, carefully cut along the dashed line, cutting away the top layer of fabric only. Clip around the curves and at the points just up to, but not quite touching, the solid line.

6. Using thread to match the black-and-white print, hand stitch the curved edges of the cut shape to the solid fabric. Turn the edges under as you go, using the solid traced line as a guide. Use small appliqué stitches.

7. Remove the basting stitches from the edges of the square, and then cut away the excess solid fabric, leaving about a ⅜" seam allowance around the hand-stitched shape.

8. Repeat steps 3–7 with the remaining three fabric squares.

▶ I kept the quilting simple by stitching on both sides of each seam, then echoing the petal shapes.

PIECING AND QUILTING THE POT HOLDER

1 Arrange the four blocks as shown and sew them into two rows. Press the seam allowances in opposite directions. Join the rows and press the seam allowances to one side or open as desired.

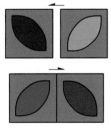

2 Layer the 11" backing square (right side down), the 11" square of cotton batting, and the 11" square of Insul-Bright. Center the pot-holder front on top as shown. Baste or pin the layers together.

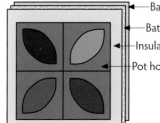

— Backing

— Batting

— Insulated batting

— Pot holder front

3 Quilt as desired. Then square up and trim excess batting and backing even with the quilted pot holder.

ADDING THE BIAS BINDING TO THE POT HOLDER

1 Enclose one raw edge of the pot holder with the bias tape, aligning one end of the bias tape with a corner. Pin or clip in place, and sew close to the inside edge of the tape, through all layers. Stop when you reach the edge of the pot holder, making sure to backstitch.

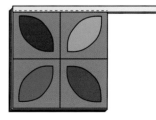

Petals Pot Holder and Trivet

2 Open the bias tape with your fingers and fold 90° to create a mitered corner as you enclose the next raw edge of the pot holder. Pin or clip in place, and then sew close to the inside edge of the tape as you did before, stopping at the edge of the pot holder and backstitching.

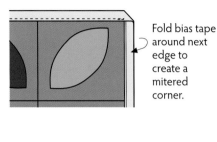

Fold bias tape around next edge to create a mitered corner.

3 Repeat the mitering of the corners and stitching until you get to the fourth side. Before sewing the tape in place on the fourth side, trim the bias tape so that you have enough to sew the last side plus 8½" for a hanging loop as shown.

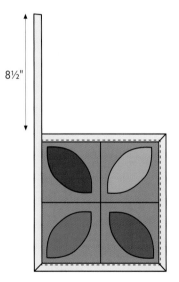

8½"

4 Open the bias tape completely at the short raw end you just trimmed and fold under ½"; close the tape again and press. Pin the end of the bias tape closed. Sew close to the inside edge of the tape all the way to the end of the tail, turning to sew the short end closed as well.

5 Create a loop by turning the extended tail of the tape around to the back side of the pot holder about ¾" as shown. Hand or machine stitch to secure the tape.

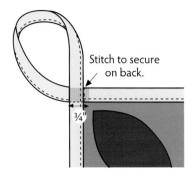

Stitch to secure on back.

¾"

ASSEMBLING THE TRIVET BLOCKS

All seam allowances are ¼". Follow instructions for "Assembling the Pot-Holder Blocks" on page 48.

1 Make four 5" petal blocks: three chartreuse and one tangerine.

2 Use the seven 3½" squares and the small petal template to make six 3½" petal blocks: one chartreuse, two tangerine, and four turquoise.

3 Use the 6½" squares and the large petal template to make one red 6½" petal block.

PIECING AND QUILTING THE TRIVET

1 Sew the blocks together as shown in the assembly diagram. Press the seam allowances in the direction of the arrows.

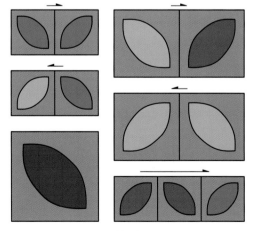

Assembly diagram

A Bit of Appliqué

2 Layer the 15" x 18" backing piece (right side down), the 15" x 18" piece of cotton batting, and the 15" x 18" piece of Insul-Bright. Center the trivet front on top, right side up. Baste or pin the layers together.

3 Quilt as desired. Then trim excess batting and backing even with the quilted trivet.

ADDING THE BIAS BINDING TO THE TRIVET

1 Starting in the middle of one side, enclose one raw edge of the trivet with the bias tape. Pin or clip in place, and sew close to the inside edge of the tape, through all layers. Stop when you reach the edge of the trivet, making sure to backstitch.

2 Open the bias tape with your fingers and fold 90° to create a mitered corner as you enclose the next raw edge of the trivet. (Refer to the illustration in step 2 of "Adding the Bias Binding to the Pot Holder" on page 49.) Pin or clip in place, and then sew close to the inside edge of the tape as you did before, stopping at the edge of the trivet and backstitching.

3 Continue in the same manner around all edges of the trivet, until you get close to the point where you started. Trim the bias tape 1½" beyond the starting point. Open the bias tape completely at the short raw end and fold under ½", and then close the tape again and press. Finish sewing the bias tape in place, covering the beginning raw end with the folded, finished end.

Medium

Large

Small

Geometric THROW PILLOW

One of the great things about using felt for appliqué is that the edges don't fray. A grid of felt shapes (not quite circles, yet not quite squares) are "appliquéd" to the pillow by way of quilted vertical, horizontal, and diagonal lines—the edges of the shapes aren't otherwise stitched down. There's a lot of geometry in finishing this pillow, and, if you enjoy precise quilting, this is the project for you to hone your skills.

▶ **FINISHED PILLOW:** 16" x 16"

▶ **TECHNIQUE:** Raw-edge felt appliqué

MATERIALS

Cotton yardage is based on 42"-wide fabric; wool felt is based on 26"-wide fabric.

⅝ yard of chartreuse cotton solid
⅝ yard of cotton print for pillow back and binding
¼ yard of medium-gray wool felt for appliqués
19" square of lightweight cotton batting
19" square of muslin*
Chartreuse all-purpose thread (or top-stitching thread to match fabric)
16" x 16" pillow form
Walking foot
Water-soluble marker
Painter's tape (optional)

Any cotton fabric will do, as this is simply a backing layer for the quilted pillow front and won't be visible in the finished pillow.

CUTTING

Make freezer-paper templates for the wool felt using the pattern on page 55.

From the chartreuse solid, cut:
1 square, 17" x 17"

From the cotton print, cut:
2 rectangles, 12" x 16½"
2 strips, 2¼" x 42"

From the gray felt, cut:
16 rounded squares

MAKING THE PILLOW FRONT

1 Mark along the raw edges on each side of the pillow front according to the measurements shown.

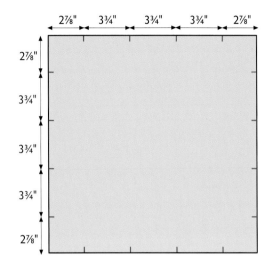

2 Fold the fabric along one pair of marks (opposite each other) and finger-press. Repeat with each pair of marks to create a grid of creases that will serve as a guide for placing the felt shapes.

3 Position one felt shape at each intersection of creases, centering each shape on the horizontal and vertical crease. Pin or hand baste the felt shapes in place.

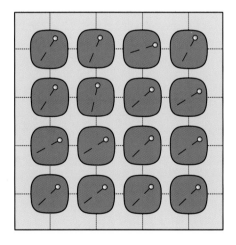

4 Make a quilt sandwich by layering the batting on top of the muslin, and then centering the pillow top on the batting, right side up. Pin or thread baste the layers together.

+ Quilting the Grid

You'll need to be fairly precise with the quilted grid lines if you want them all to intersect in the centers of the felt shapes. If your creased lines have begun to disappear, you can draw them in again using a clear acrylic ruler and water-soluble marker. Just connect the opposing marks as you did in the first steps. I don't recommend marking on the felt itself (only on the cotton fabric) unless you test the marker on the felt first to be sure it will fade completely. Or, instead of marking the fabric, you can use lengths of painter's tape as guidelines for your stitching. Just place the edge of the tape right next to an original crease line, and sew next to the edge. When you're done, gently remove the tape.

---

5 With a walking foot on your machine and thread to match the pillow front fabric, quilt a grid of vertical and horizontal lines on the creases you made in the pillow front. If the creases are hard to see, refer to "Quilting the Grid" above for some suggestions. Take your time when stitching, and hold down the edges of the felt shapes to make sure they don't shift as you approach them with the presser foot.

A Bit of Appliqué

▶ **The quilted lines are both decorative and functional.**

1 Fold and press ½" to the wrong side along one 16½" edge of a print 12" x 16½" backing rectangle. Fold and press an additional ½" to the wrong side along the same edge. Pin the hem in place. Repeat with the second backing rectangle.

2 Using matching thread, sew the hem by topstitching ⅜" from the outer-folded edge of both rectangles to make the back panels.

3 Lay the pillow front on a flat surface with the right side down. Lay the back panels on the pillow front with the right sides up and all raw edges aligned. The hemmed edges of the back panels will overlap by about 5" at the center. Pin the panels in place, and then turn the pillow over so the front is facing up.

4 Using the print 2¼" x 42" strips, prepare and sew the binding to the pillow. If you're unfamiliar with how to make and attach binding to a project, see ShopMartingale.com/HowtoQuilt for free illustrated information.

5 Insert the pillow form through the overlapped edges on the pillow back.

6 Using painter's tape or a water-soluble marker, mark diagonal lines on the pillow top by connecting the points of the intersecting horizontal and vertical stitching. Also mark parallel diagonal lines through each corner felt shape. Stitch the marked diagonal lines as before.

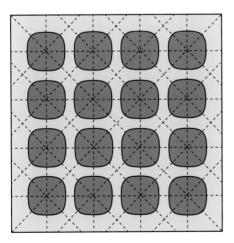

7 Remove any basting stitches or pins. Trim and square up the pillow top to 16½" x 16½".

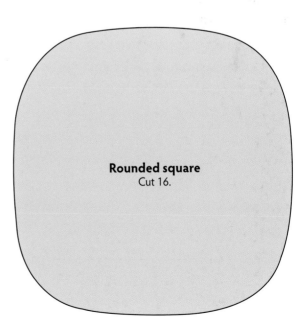

Rounded square
Cut 16.

Spot-On COASTERS

Quilted coasters highlight a colorful strip-pieced circle and an easy appliqué technique. There's no need to fear the circle: once you learn the simple method of gathering the fabric around a circle template, you may not be able to stop making these. The appliqué is quickly attached with machine stitching—no hand sewing required!

▶ **FINISHED COASTERS:** 4½" x 4½"
▶ **TECHNIQUE:** Gathered-circle appliqué

MATERIALS FOR 4 COASTERS

Yardage is based on 42"-wide fabric.

¼ yard or 1 fat quarter (18" x 21") of dark-gray linen/cotton blend (or cotton print) for coaster fronts and backs

⅛ yard or 2 squares, 5" x 5", *each* of 4 coordinating cotton prints for pieced appliqués

4 squares, 5½" x 5½", of low-loft cotton batting

Cardstock for circle template*

You can use a cereal box from the recycling bin or whatever you have on hand.

CUTTING

From the dark-gray linen/cotton blend fabric, cut:
8 squares, 5" x 5"

From *each* of the coordinating prints, cut:
8 strips, 1" x 5" (32 total)

PIECING THE CIRCLES

All seam allowances are ¼".

1 Sew one 1" x 5" strip of each color together along the long edges to make a 2½" x 5" strip set. Press the seam allowances to one side. Repeat with a second set of four strips. Cut each strip set in half crosswise to make two squares, 2½" x 2½".

2½"   2½"

Cut.

4 Repeat steps 1–3 with the remaining fabric strips to make a total of four gathered circles.

FINISHING THE COASTERS

1 Center a patchwork circle on a dark-gray 5" square. Pin the circle in place, and topstitch close to the edge.

2 Center the appliquéd square, right side up, on top of a 5½" square of cotton batting. Quilt as desired, and then trim to 5" x 5".

3 Place the quilted coaster top on a dark-gray 5" square, right sides together. Sew around all sides using a ¼" seam allowance, leaving a 2" opening at the center of one side.

4 Trim the corners diagonally to reduce bulk. Turn the coaster right side out through the opening and gently push out the corners. Press, turning the seam allowances to the inside at the opening. Hand stitch the opening closed.

5 Topstitch close to the edge around all sides.

6 Repeat steps 1–5 for the remaining three coasters.

+ **Mix It Up**

For a scrappier patchwork look, mix up the order of the prints for the second set of strips.

2 Arrange the four squares as shown and then sew together in pairs. Press the seam allowances in opposite directions. Join the pairs and press the seam allowances to one side.

3 From the patchwork square, make a 3½"-diameter gathered circle, referring to "Gathered-Circle Appliqué" on page 11.

+ **Easy Templates**

A wide-mouth mason jar ring is almost exactly 3½" in diameter and works well for creating the circle template needed, or use the circle pattern provided on this page.

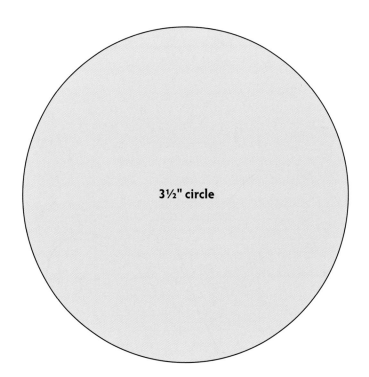

3½" circle

Circles BABY QUILT

Two simple Bull's-Eye block patterns combine for a colorful and graphic baby quilt. This version was made with super-soft flannel in assorted polka dots. The raw-edge circle appliqués take a bit of time to prepare, but then the quilt comes together quickly.

▶ **FINISHED QUILT:** 36½" x 36½"
▶ **FINISHED BLOCKS:** 10" x 10"
▶ **TECHNIQUE:** Raw-edge fusible appliqué

MATERIALS

Yardage is based on 42"-wide fabric. Use cotton OR cotton flannel for each cut of fabric.

1 yard of light-yellow print for blocks
¾ yard of aqua polka dot for blocks
¾ yard of lime polka dot for blocks
⅔ yard of orange polka dot for blocks and border
⅓ yard of orange solid for binding
1⅓ yards of fabric for backing
40" x 40" square of cotton batting
All-purpose thread to match fabric
2¾ yards of 18"-wide lightweight fusible web
Cardstock for templates

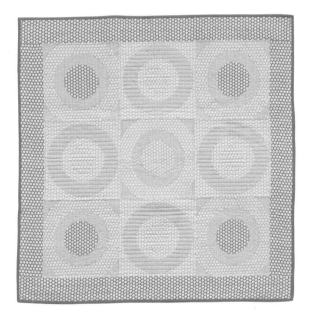

▶ "Circles Baby Quilt"

CUTTING

From the light-yellow print, cut:
9 squares, 10½" x 10½"

From the orange polka dot, cut:
4 squares, 5½" x 5½"
4 strips, 3½" x 42"

From the aqua polka dot, cut:
4 squares, 10½" x 10½"
1 square, 5½" x 5½"

From the lime polka dot, cut:
5 squares, 10½" x 10½"

From the orange solid, cut:
4 strips, 2¼" x 42"

From the fabric for backing, cut:
1 square, 40" x 40"

From the fusible web, cut:
9 squares, 10¼" x 10¼"
5 squares, 5¼" x 5¼"

PREPARING THE APPLIQUÉS

1 Trace the patterns on pages 64 and 65 onto cardstock and carefully cut them out.

2 Fuse the 10¼" squares of fusible web to the wrong side of the 10½" squares of fabric in the following colors and quantities: four aqua, four yellow, and one lime. Leave the paper backing attached.

3 Fuse the 5¼" squares of fusible web to the wrong side of the five 5½" squares of fabric: four orange and one aqua. Leave the paper backing attached.

4 Fold one 10½" square of aqua fabric in half, with wrong (paper) sides together. Align the raw edges, finger-press to crease folds, and then unfold it. Fold the square in half in the opposite direction, aligning raw edges and finger-pressing to crease again. Lay the square so the right side of the fabric is facing down and the paper side of the fusible web is facing up. Draw a small plus

sign with a marker or pencil in the center, at the intersection of the creases, to help with aligning the templates.

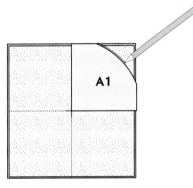

5 Position template A1 in one quadrant of the aqua square so that the 90° corner is aligned with the intersection of creases (the "+" you marked), and the straight sides are aligned with two creases. Trace along the curved edge of the template with a marker or pencil.

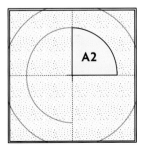

6 Place the template in another quadrant and repeat step 5. Repeat to trace the template in each of the four quadrants.

7 On the same square of fabric, position and trace template A2 in the same manner. After drawing the curve in the first quadrant, you can use it to help align the template in the subsequent quadrants.

8 Place template B3 in the center of the same square, aligning the marks on the template with the creases, and trace. You have now traced the outer ring for block A and the inner circle for block B.

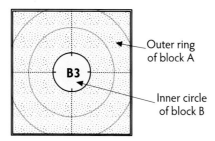

Outer ring of block A

Inner circle of block B

9 Repeat steps 4–8 for the remaining three aqua 10½" squares.

10 Repeat steps 4–7 to trace templates A1 and A2 on the paper side of the lime 10½" square.

11 Repeat steps 4–7 to trace templates B1 and B2 on the paper side of four yellow 10½" squares.

12 Follow step 4 to fold and crease the five 5½" squares in the same way that you did with the larger squares. Center and trace template A3 on the paper side of each of these smaller squares.

13 Cut out all of the rings and circles along the lines you traced, and carefully remove the paper backing. Keep the pieces as shown and discard the remainder.

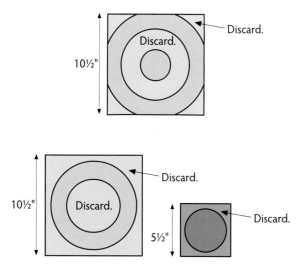

Discard.

Discard.

10½"

Discard.

Discard.

10½"

Discard.

5½"

Discard.

APPLIQUÉING BLOCK A

1 Fold one yellow 10½" square in half. Align the raw edges, finger-press to crease the folds, and then unfold it. Fold the square in half in the opposite direction, aligning raw edges and finger-pressing to crease again. Unfold the square and lay it out with the right side up.

2 Lay one aqua outer ring on the square, matching raw edges and creases. Lay one orange circle in the center of the square, using the creases as a guide. Fuse the appliqués (outer ring and inner circle) to the fabric.

3 Repeat steps 1 and 2 to make three more blocks. To make the center block A, repeat steps 1 and 2 with the last yellow 10½" square, the lime outer ring, and the larger aqua inner circle.

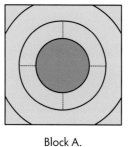 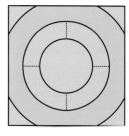

Block A.
Make 4.

Center block A.
Make 1.

4 Using a straight stitch, sew close to the edges of the appliqué rings and circles to secure them to the backgrounds.

+ Zipper Foot Help

You may want to switch out your regular sewing-machine foot for a zipper foot. While its main purpose is for installing zippers, this foot works well when stitching the appliqués to maintain an even distance from the raw edges of the rings and circles. Align the edge of the zipper foot with the raw edge of the appliqué shape to help you maintain an even distance from the edge.

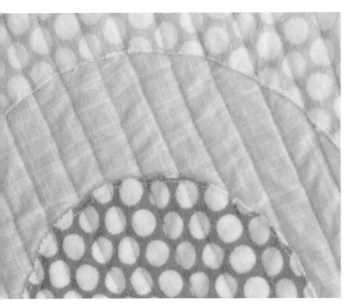

▶ The raw edges of the appliqués will fray slightly with use, lending subtle texture to the quilt's surface.

APPLIQUÉING BLOCK B

1 Fold one lime 10½" square in half. Align the raw edges, finger-press to crease the folds, and then unfold it. Fold the square in half in the opposite direction, aligning raw edges and finger-pressing to crease again. Unfold the square and lay it out with the right side up.

2 Lay one yellow outer ring on the square, matching the creases to center it. Lay one aqua circle in the center of the square, again using the creases as a guide. Fuse the appliqués (outer ring and inner circle) to the fabric. Make a total of four blocks.

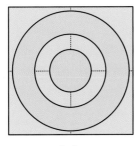

Block B.
Make 4.

3 Using a straight stitch, sew close to the edges of the appliqué rings and circles to secure them to the backgrounds.

FINISHING THE QUILT

1 Sew the completed blocks together in a nine-patch pattern as shown in the quilt assembly diagram below. Press the seam allowances away from block A to reduce bulk, or press open.

2 Measure the width of the quilt top through the center and cut two of the orange polka-dot 3½" x 42" strips to that measurement. Sew the strips to the top and bottom of the quilt. Press the seam allowances toward the border. Measure the length of the quilt through center, including the borders just added. Trim the remaining two orange strips to that length and sew them to the sides of the quilt. Press the seam allowances toward the border.

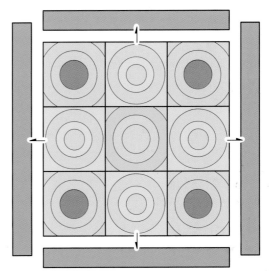

Quilt assembly

3 Make a quilt sandwich by placing the backing right side down and layering the batting on top. Center the quilt top on the batting, right side up. Pin or thread baste the layers together.

4 Quilt as desired. Then trim excess batting and backing even with the quilt top.

5 Using the orange-solid 2¼" x 42" strips, prepare and sew the binding to the quilt. If you're unfamiliar with how to make and attach binding, go to ShopMartingale.com/HowtoQuilt for free illustrated information.

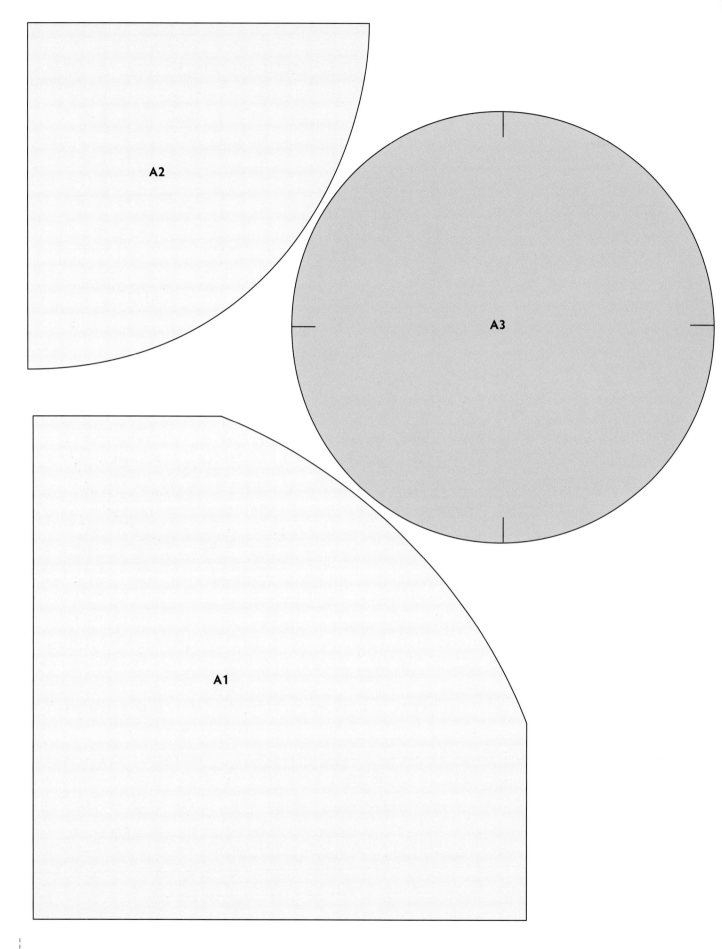

A2

A3

A1

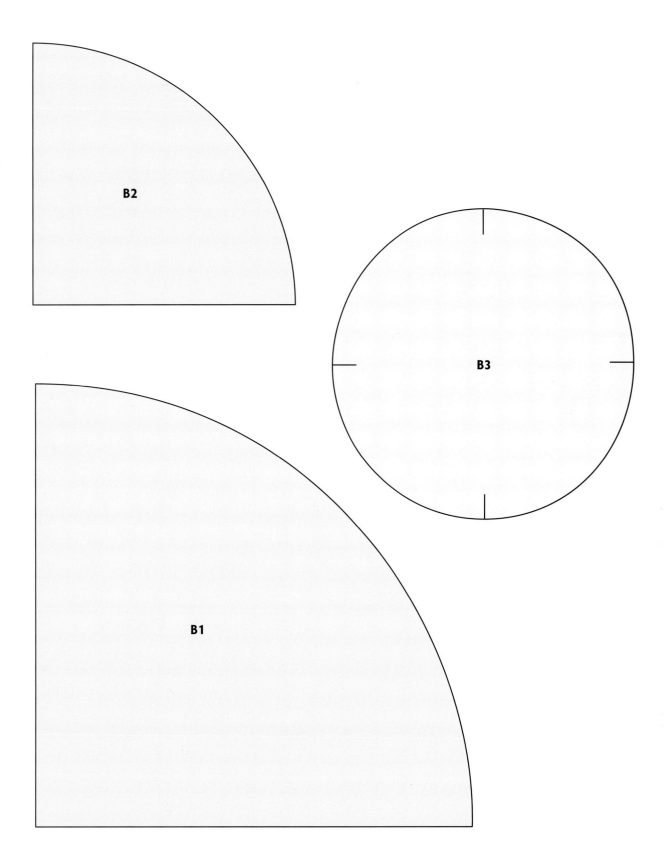

B2

B3

B1

Polly THE PENGUIN SOFTIE

Adorably soft and cuddly, Polly might come from a cold climate, but she will surely warm your heart. Choose a classic tweed fabric and sturdy wool felt for her body and features. Then add a playful cotton print for her belly.

▶ **FINISHED PENGUIN:** 9" x 11"
▶ **TECHNIQUES:** Raw-edge fusible appliqué and raw-edge felt appliqué

MATERIALS

Wool yardage is based on 54"-wide fabric.

⅜ yard of wool or wool-blend tweed for the body and wings
9" x 9" piece of cotton print for belly appliqué
8" x 8" piece of dark-purple wool felt for feet
3" x 6" piece of teal wool felt for eyes
3" x 3" piece of mustard wool felt for beak
2" x 3" piece of black wool felt for pupils
9" x 12" piece of fusible web
Polyester stuffing (12 ounce bag)
Freezer paper

CUTTING

Using the patterns on pages 69–71, trace the body and wing patterns onto paper or freezer paper and cut out the shapes to make pattern templates. Trace the foot pattern onto freezer paper.

From the wool tweed, cut:
2 bodies
2 wings
2 wings reversed

From the dark-purple felt, cut:
4 feet

EMBELLISHING THE PENGUIN

1 Using the patterns on pages 69 and 72, trace the belly, two eyes, two pupils, and a beak onto the paper side of fusible web. Cut around the shapes at least ¼" away from the traced lines.

2 Fuse the belly pattern to the wrong side of the cotton print. Fuse the eyes to the teal felt, the pupils to the black felt, and the beak to the mustard felt. Cut the shapes out on the drawn lines and remove the paper backing.

3 Using the body pattern as a guide, position the belly on the penguin front. Following the manufacturer's instructions, fuse the appliqué in place.

▶ Take your time while sewing around the curves of the smaller appliqué shapes.

4 Using a straight stitch and matching thread, topstitch 1/16" to 1/8" from the edge of the appliqué.

+ Securing the Stitches

Instead of backstitching to secure my stitches when attaching the appliqué shapes, I like to leave the thread ends at least 2" long and pull them to the back when I've finished. Then I tie them together by hand before trimming. This takes a few minutes longer than backstitching, but ensures that each piece is firmly attached.

---

5 Using the body pattern as a guide, position the eyes, beak, and pupils on the penguin front. Fuse the appliqués in place.

6 Using a straight stitch and matching thread, topstitch 1/16" to 1/8" from the edge of the appliqué shapes.

ASSEMBLING THE FEET AND WINGS

1 Pin two foot pieces together, matching up all edges.

2 Using a straight stitch and matching thread, topstitch 1/8" from the edges, leaving the top edge open, to create a double-layered foot.

Topstitch 1/8" from edge.

3 Repeat with the two remaining foot pieces.

4 Using a 1/4" seam allowance, sew two wing pieces around the curved edges, right sides together, leaving the short straight edge open. Clip the curves and turn the wing right side out. Repeat with the remaining two wing pieces.

5 Lightly fill the wings with stuffing.

ASSEMBLING THE PENGUIN

1 Lay the penguin front flat, right side up. Using the marks on the pattern as a guide, pin the feet upside down to the body so the tops of the feet align with the bottom edge of the body. Then pin the wings to the body as shown.

2 Lay the penguin back piece on top, right sides together, and pin around the edges. Using a ¼" seam allowance, stitch around the edges, leaving a 4" opening below one of the wings for turning. Reinforce the wings and feet by sewing again within the seam allowance, close to the first line of stitching.

3 Clip the curves, and then turn the penguin right side out through the opening. Use a point turner, knitting needle, or similar tool to carefully push out the bottom corners.

4 Fill the penguin with stuffing. Then turn the seam allowances to the inside at the opening and pin closed. Hand stitch the opening closed using matching thread and a slipstitch.

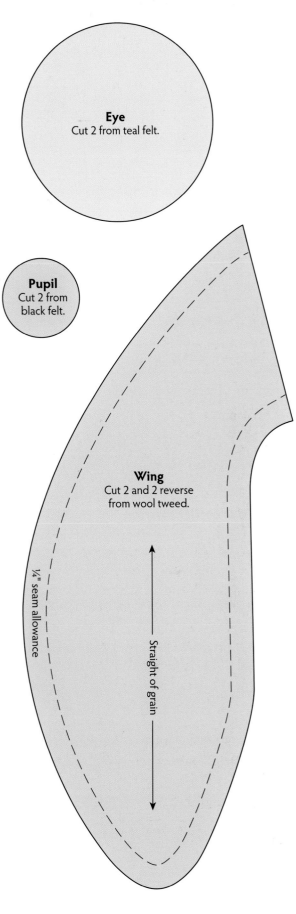

Eye
Cut 2 from teal felt.

Pupil
Cut 2 from black felt.

Wing
Cut 2 and 2 reverse from wool tweed.

¼" seam allowance

Straight of grain

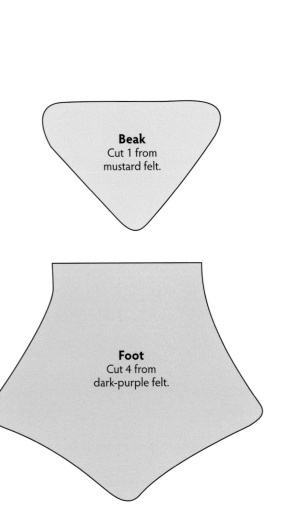

Beak
Cut 1 from mustard felt.

Foot
Cut 4 from dark-purple felt.

Foot location

Foot location

Match to complete pattern.

Wing location

Match to complete pattern.

¼" seam allowance

Body
Cut 2 from
wool tweed.

Wing location

Belly
Cut 1 from
cotton print.

A Bit of Appliqué

Directional MESSENGER BAG

*A **perfect combination of style and utility,** this graphic bag is built for a day on the go. Two exterior pockets—one perfectly sized for a water bottle—a roomy interior with additional pockets, a clip for your keys, and a sturdy denim exterior add plenty of functionality.*

▶ **FINISHED BAG:** 16" x 12" x 3"; strap is adjustable to about 46" long.

▶ **TECHNIQUE:** Raw-edge fusible appliqué

MATERIALS

Yardage is based on 42"-wide fabric.

1⅜ yards of cotton print for lining

1⅓ yards of gray denim for bag*

½ yard or 1 fat quarter (18" x 21") of cotton print for arrow appliqué

1½ yards of 20"-wide woven lightweight fusible interfacing

½ yard of 18"-wide fusible web

6" length of ¾"-wide elastic

8" length of fusible hook-and-loop tape (such as Velcro Fabric Fusion)

Parachute buckle (with reflective center, if desired) for 1½"-wide strap

Bar slide buckle for 1½"-wide strap

1" swivel lobster clasp or snap hook

*You can also use canvas or duck cloth if you prefer.

CUTTING

From the gray denim, cut:

2 rectangles, 13" x 17", for front and back panels

1 rectangle, 14" x 17", for flap

1 strip, 4" x 40½", for sides/bottom panel

1 strip, 2½" x 13", for strap

1 strip, 2½" x 40", for strap

1 rectangle, 8" x 11", for gathered side pocket

1 rectangle, 5" x 8", for flat side pocket

From the cotton print for lining, cut:

2 rectangles, 13" x 17", for front- and back-panel lining

2 rectangles, 14" x 17", for flap lining and interior pocket

1 strip, 4" x 40½", for sides/bottom lining

1 strip, 2½" x 13", for strap lining

1 strip, 2½" x 40", for strap lining

1 rectangle, 8" x 11", for pocket lining

1 rectangle, 5" x 8", for pocket lining

1 rectangle, 3½" x 5", for key tab

From the interfacing, cut:

2 rectangles, 12½" x 16½", for front and back panels

1 rectangle, 13½" x 16½", for front flap

1 strip, 3½" x 40", for sides/bottom panel

PREPARING THE BAG PIECES

1 Referring to "Applying Fusible Interfacing" on page 15, center and fuse interfacing to the denim 13" x 17" front and back panels, the denim 4" x 40½" sides/bottom panel, and the denim 14" x 17" front flap.

2 Make a template from paper or cardstock using the pattern on page 80. Use it to round the bottom corners of the denim 13" x 17" front and back panels and the denim 14" x 17" front flap. Cut the top corners of the denim front flap as shown.

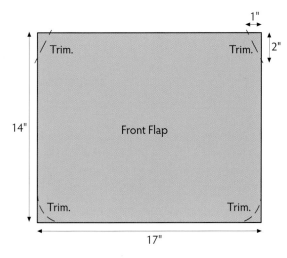

3 Repeat step 2 with the lining pieces.

4 Cut the long sides of the denim 5" x 8" flat side pocket and print 5" x 8" pocket-lining piece at an angle as shown to create trapezoid shapes.

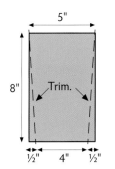

ADDING THE APPLIQUÉ

1 Trace the arrow pattern on pages 79 and 80 onto the paper side of the fusible web. Cut out the shape from the fusible web, leaving a border of about ¼". Following the manufacturer's instructions, iron the fusible web to the wrong side of the appliqué fabric. Cut out the shape and remove the paper backing.

2 Place the appliqué on the right side of the denim front flap and fuse the appliqué in place.

3 Using a small zigzag stitch, sew along the raw edges of the appliqué to secure them. There's no need to stitch along the top, bottom, and side raw edges, as they will be enclosed in the seam allowance later.

PREPARING THE FLAP AND POCKETS

All seam allowances are ½".

1 With right sides together, sew the appliquéd flap and flap lining together along the sides and bottom, leaving the top open for turning. Clip the curves and corners, turn the flap right side out and press. Topstitch ⅛" from the finished edges and machine baste ¼" from the raw edges.

2 To prepare the flat side pocket, place the trapezoid-shaped denim pocket and lining pieces right sides together with raw edges aligned. Sew the pieces together along the two short sides only. Turn the pocket right side out, press, and topstitch ¼" from the two finished edges.

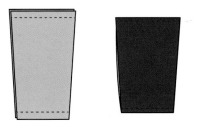

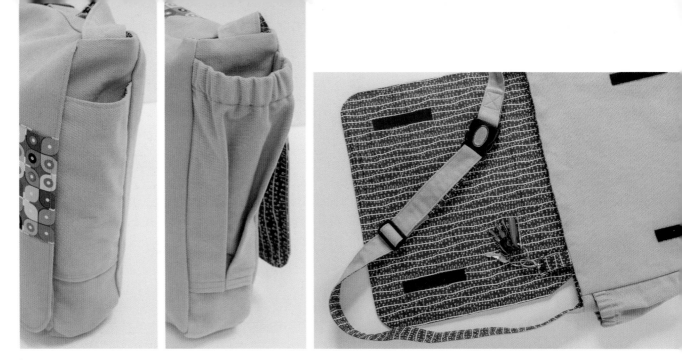

▶ Multiple pockets and a key clip make this bag super functional.

3 To prepare the gathered side pocket, place the denim 8" x 11" rectangle right sides together with the print 8" x 11" lining rectangle and sew along one 8" side. Turn the pocket right side out and press the sewn edge. With wrong sides together, machine baste ¼" from the raw edges along the opposite, unfinished 8" side, through both denim and lining.

4 Fold the basted 8" edge under ½" toward the lining side and press. Fold an additional 1" and press again; then pin the folds in place. Sew ⅛" from the inside folded edge to create a casing for the elastic.

5 Fold the same pocket in half lengthwise, so the lining is facing out. Make a mark 2" from the fold along the bottom finished edge (not the casing side), and then sew a short vertical line of stitches at this mark, about ½" long, from the finished edge. Make sure to backstitch.

6 Open the pocket and, with the right side out, flatten the lower edge to create an inverted box pleat. Press, and then sew the box pleat in place by topstitching ¼" from the finished edge, across the pleat.

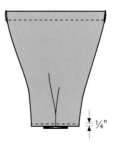

7 Feed the elastic into the casing of the pocket and pin at both ends. Sew ¼" from the raw edges, across both ends of the elastic, to secure.

MAKING THE BAG

1 Pin the pockets to the denim 4" x 40½" sides/ bottom panel, measuring 10½" from each end as shown. Baste the pockets in place ¼" from the raw edges through all layers. Sew along the bottom of each pocket, ⅛" above the topstitching.

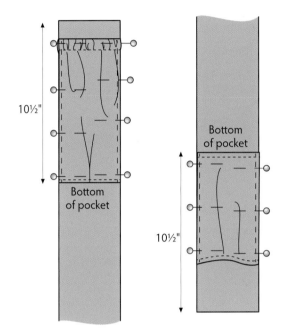

2 Pin the denim sides/bottom panel to the front panel, with right sides together, starting at one top corner of the front panel, and pinning all the way along the sides, curved bottom corners, and bottom to the opposite top corner. Pin often at the curves to keep the fabric from bunching up. Sew around the sides and bottom. Repeat to sew the unit to the denim back panel. Set aside.

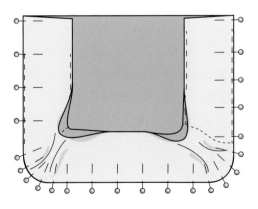

3 Place the denim 2½" x 13" strap right sides together with the print 2½" x 13" lining piece. Pin the strap pieces together with raw edges aligned. Sew along one long side, one short side, and 2" on the next long side as shown. Trim the corners, turn the strap right side out and press, also turning under and pressing ½" of the unsewn length of the long sides. Repeat with the 2½" x 40" denim and lining strips. Topstitch close to the finished and folded edges of both straps. Note: Sewing the straps in this manner avoids having to turn a long tube right side out.

4 Feed the finished end of the shorter strap through the male part of the parachute buckle and fold 2½" to the wrong side. Pin the strap in place, and sew it closed by stitching a square with an "X" inside.

5 Feed the finished end of the longer strap through the bar slide buckle, the female part of the parachute buckle, and then back through the bar slide buckle. Fold the strap 2½" to the wrong side and pin it in place. Sew the strap closed by stitching a square with an "X" inside.

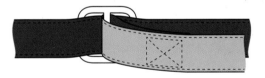

MAKING THE LINING

1 For the interior pocket, fold the print 14" x 17" lining rectangle in half crosswise, with right sides together, matching up the 14" sides. Sew around the three raw edges, leaving a 3" opening in the long side for turning. Trim the corners, turn the pocket right side out, and press, turning the seam allowances to the inside at the opening. Topstitch ⅛" from the folded edge.

2 Pin the pocket to the right side of the print 13" x 17" back-panel lining so the topstitched edge is 3" from the top edge of the back-panel lining and centered horizontally. Sew around the sides and bottom of the pocket, ⅛" from edges and leaving the top open. Backstitch at the top edges to reinforce the pocket opening.

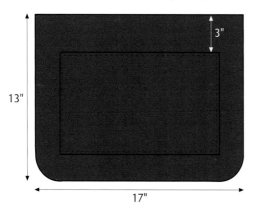

3 Pin the print 4" x 40½" sides/bottom lining to the print 13" x 17" front-panel lining, with right sides together, starting at one top corner of the front panel, and pinning all the way along the sides, curved bottom corners, and bottom to the opposite top corner. Pin often at the curves to keep the fabric from bunching up. Sew around the sides and bottom. Repeat to sew the unit to the back-panel lining. Set aside.

4 Fold the print 3½" x 5" rectangle in half lengthwise, wrong sides together, and press. Open the rectangle, fold each long edge to the center, and press again. Fold again along the first fold to enclose the raw edges and press again. This will create a tab about ⅞" wide and 5" long. Topstitch close to each long edge.

5 Feed the tab through the base of the lobster clasp or swivel hook, and fold it in half. Pin near the raw edges.

FINISHING THE BAG

1 Pin the flap to the denim back panel with the denim sides together and raw edges aligned. Pin one strap to each side of the bag with denim sides together, raw edges aligned, and centered on the side panels. Pin the tab with the swivel hook to the denim front panel, 2½" from the side seam, with raw edges aligned. Baste the flap, straps, and tab to the denim bag ¼" from the raw edges.

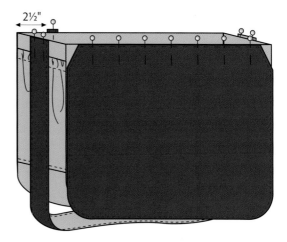

2 Place the denim bag inside the lining with right sides together. Make sure the flap, straps, and tab are tucked in between the layers. Align all seams and raw edges, and pin the layers in place.

3 Sew the lining and bag together, leaving a 9" opening at the front of the bag for turning. Sew again at each strap location, stitching within the seam allowance and close to the first seam, to reinforce the straps.

4 Turn the bag right side out through the opening. Press along the seam, turning the seam allowances to the inside at the opening. Topstitch close to the finished seam, or hand sew the opening closed with a slipstitch. If desired, tack the tab to the lining side of the bag with a few small hand stitches.

5 Cut the hook-and-loop tape into two 4" lengths. Following the manufacturer's instructions, fuse the hook-and-loop tape to the lining side of the flap and the denim side of the bag front as desired. I positioned it vertically, one length on each side, about 2" or so from the side seams and bottom edge. See the photo on page 76.

A Bit of Appliqué

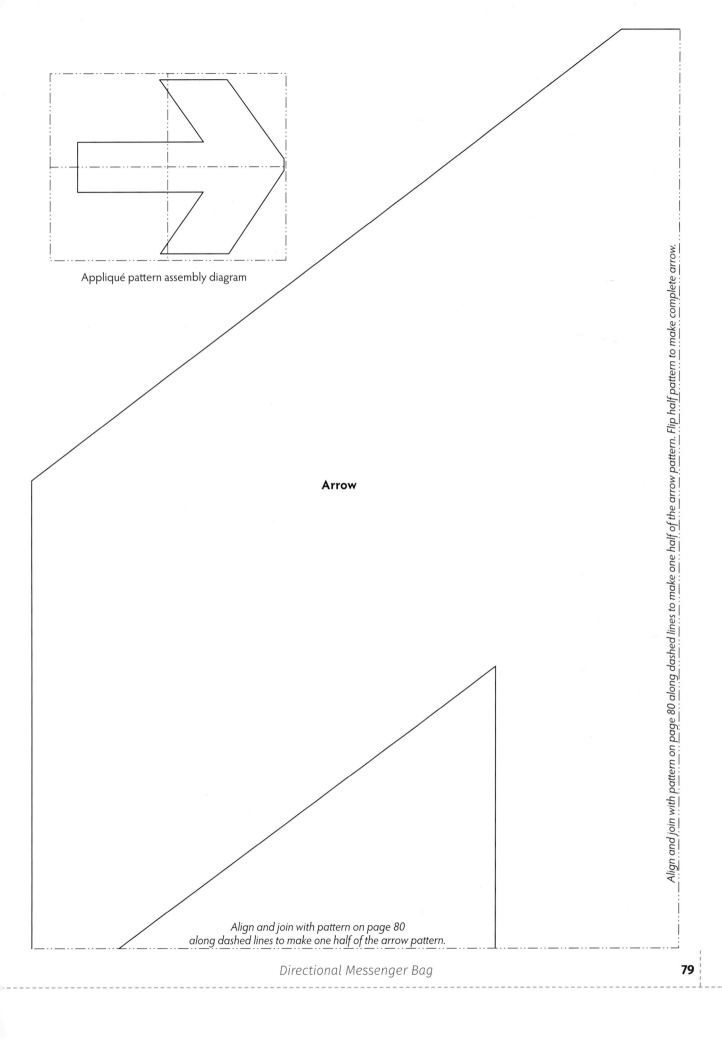

Appliqué pattern assembly diagram

Arrow

*Align and join with pattern on page 80
along dashed lines to make one half of the arrow pattern.*

Align and join with pattern on page 80 along dashed lines to make one half of the arrow pattern. Flip half pattern to make complete arrow.

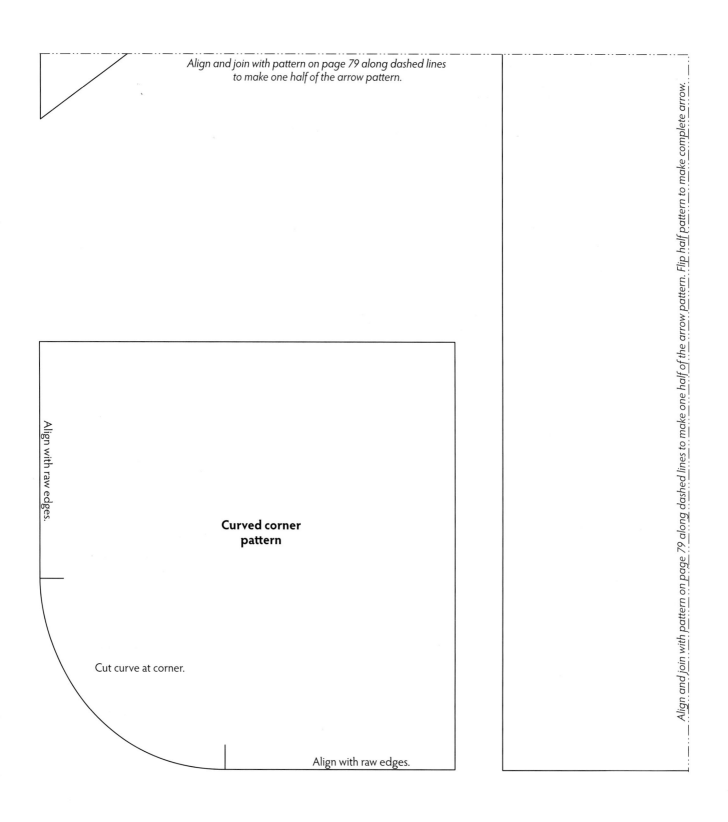

Align and join with pattern on page 79 along dashed lines to make one half of the arrow pattern.

Align with raw edges.

Curved corner pattern

Cut curve at corner.

Align with raw edges.

Align and join with pattern on page 79 along dashed lines to make one half of the arrow pattern. Flip half pattern to make complete arrow.

Sewing Love
POUCH AND PINCUSHION

Go ahead. Show the world, or at least your friends, just how much you love to sew. This adorable Zakka-style pouch and pincushion set features tiny felt appliqués and fun embroidered details that illustrate your devotion to handcrafts. The pouch is perfect for storing your embroidery, English paper piecing, or small hand-sewing projects.

▶ **FINISHED POUCH:** 9" x 6" x 2"

▶ **FINISHED PINCUSHION:** 3½" x 5"

▶ **TECHNIQUES:** Raw-edge felt appliqué, and embroidery

MATERIALS FOR POUCH AND PINCUSHION

Yardage is based on 42"-wide fabric.

⅜ yard of cotton print for pouch and pincushion accent, pouch lining, and pocket piping

⅜ yard of cotton solid for pouch interior pockets

¼ yard of natural linen/cotton blend fabric for pouch and pincushion

2" x 3" piece of mustard wool felt for heart appliqué

2" x 4" piece of teal wool felt for sewing needle appliqué

2 rectangles, 7½" x 10¾", of fusible fleece for pouch interfacing

2 rectangles, 7¼" x 10¼", of woven fusible interfacing for pouch lining*

9"-long zipper for pouch

Water-soluble marker

Polyester stuffing for pincushion

Embroidery floss in several coordinating colors**

All-purpose thread in colors to match felt

Zipper foot

5" length of narrow satin ribbon for zipper pull (optional)

This interfacing is optional, but it makes the interior nice and sturdy for holding scissors and other sewing items.

**I used six different colors for the pincushion, and one for the pouch.*

CUTTING FOR THE POUCH

From the linen, cut:
2 rectangles, 5" x 10¾"

From the print, cut:
2 rectangles, 4" x 10¾"
2 rectangles, 7¾" x 10¾"
2 rectangles, 2" x 2¾"
2 strips, 1¼" x 9½"

From the solid, cut:
2 rectangles, 9½" x 10"

From the teal felt, cut:
1 sewing needle shape

From the mustard felt, cut:
1 heart shape

CUTTING FOR PINCUSHION

From the linen, cut:
1 rectangle, 4½" x 6"
1 rectangle, 4½" x 4"

From the print, cut:
1 rectangle, 4½" x 3"

From the mustard felt, cut:
1 heart shape

MAKING THE POUCH EXTERIOR

All seam allowances are ½".

1 With right sides together and raw edges of one long side aligned, sew one linen 5" x 10¾" rectangle to one print 4" x 10¾" rectangle. Press the seam allowances toward the print rectangle. On the print fabric, topstitch close to the seam. Repeat with the second linen and print rectangles.

2 Lay one of the panels from step 1 right side up. Place the appliqué shapes on the fabric, positioning the heart 2" from the bottom and left edge, and the needle above the seam. Refer to the placement guide above right. Pin the appliqués in place and hand sew them to the pouch panel using two strands of matching thread and a small appliqué stitch.

3 Mark the "thread" line with a water-soluble marker. Using three strands of embroidery floss and a backstitch, embroider the *solid* line of the thread.

4 Again, using three strands of embroidery floss, embroider the *dashed* line of the thread with a running stitch. This will be the pouch front panel.

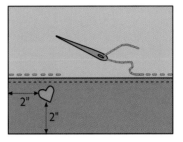

5 On the second (back) panel, embroider the dashed line of thread above the seam with a running stitch and using three strands of embroidery floss.

6 Press the front and back panels to smooth any wrinkles in the linen. Following the manufacturer's instructions, fuse the fleece to the wrong side of each panel so that it is ½" from the top edge. Press the top edge of each panel ½" to the wrong side. Set aside.

PREPARING THE POCKETS AND LINING

1 To make the flat piping for the pockets, fold the short ends of each print 1¼" x 9½" strip ½" to the wrong side and press. Then press the strip in half lengthwise, wrong sides together, to make a ⅝" x 8½" piping strip. Repeat with the second 1¼"-wide strip.

2 To make the pockets, fold one solid 9½" x 10" rectangle in half, right sides together, so the 9½"-long sides are aligned. The folded piece should measure 5" x 9½".

3 Tuck the piping strip inside the pocket along the long raw edge, centering it and aligning the raw edges with the long raw edges of the pocket. The long folded edge of the piping will be hidden inside the folded pocket. Pin the piping in

place and sew around the three raw edges of the pocket, leaving a 3" opening along one short side. Turn the pocket right side out through the opening and press, turning the seam allowances to the inside at the opening. Repeat with the second pocket and prepared piping strip.

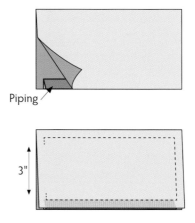

Piping

3"

4 Referring to "Applying Fusible Interfacing" on page 15, center and fuse the interfacing rectangles to the wrong side of the two print 7¾" x 10¾" lining rectangles.

5 Place a prepared pocket on the right side of each of the lining panels so they are centered horizontally, 1½" from the top edge, and 1¾" from the bottom edge. Pin the pockets in place. If you'd like the pockets to be divided, mark vertical lines on them with a water-soluble marker. Sew the pockets to the lining panels, about ⅛" from the pocket sides and bottom. Sew along the vertical dividing lines, if desired. Set the lining panels aside.

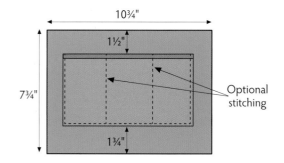

10¾"

1½"

7¾"

1¾"

Optional stitching

PREPARING THE ZIPPER

1 Fold one print 2" x 2¾" rectangle in half along the 2¾" length, wrong sides together, and press. Unfold the rectangle, fold each 2" raw edge toward the center, and press again. Fold in half once more and press to make one zipper tab, 2" x approximately ¾". Repeat with the second print 2" x 2¾" rectangle.

2 Trim the extra tape at the starting end of the zipper just above the top of the zipper teeth, and at the end of the zipper so the remaining length is 9".

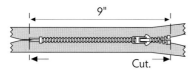

9"

Cut.

3 Place the bottom end of the zipper inside one of the folded zipper tabs, pushing it against the fold, and centering it. Topstitch close to the open edge of the zipper tab, catching all fabric layers and sewing straight across the zipper teeth to enclose the bottom end of the zipper. Open the zipper about 3" and repeat with the other zipper tab and the top of the zipper. Trim zipper tabs even with the zipper tape.

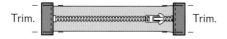

Trim.   Trim.

ATTACHING THE ZIPPER

1 Place one lining panel right side up. Center the zipper on the lining along the top, 10¾"-long edge. With the zipper closed and the zipper pull to the right, align the top edge of the zipper tape with the raw edge of the lining and pin it in place. Using a zipper foot, baste the zipper to the lining close to the raw edge.

▶ Appliqué and embroidery make this perfectly functional pouch extra special.

2 Place the lining panel right side up, with the zipper attached, so that the zipper side is toward you. Lay the pouch front on top of the zipper fabric with the folded edge of the pouch front just touching the bottom of the zipper teeth. With the zipper foot still attached, stitch through all layers (pouch front, zipper, and lining) close to the folded edge of the pouch front.

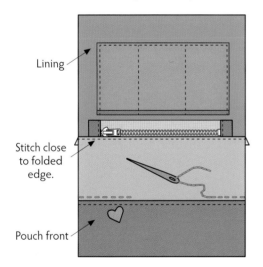

Lining

Stitch close to folded edge.

Pouch front

3 Fold the lining away from the zipper teeth and toward the wrong side of the pouch front. The wrong side of the lining will be facing the wrong side of the pouch front. Press.

+ Easy Zipper Stitching

When attaching the zipper, stop sewing with the needle in the down position when you reach the zipper pull. Raise the presser foot, carefully slide the zipper pull past the needle, and then lower the foot and continue sewing.

4 Place the second lining panel right side up. Center the zipper (with the pouch front and lining attached) on the lining along the top, 10¾"-long edge. With the zipper closed and the zipper pull to the left, align the top edge of the zipper tape with the raw edge of the lining and pin it in place. Using a zipper foot, baste the zipper to the lining close to the raw edge.

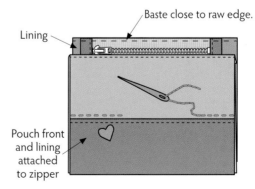

Baste close to raw edge.

Lining

Pouch front and lining attached to zipper

5 Place the newly added lining panel right side up, with the zipper and pouch front attached, so that the zipper side is toward you. Lay the pouch back piece on top of the zipper fabric with the folded edge of the pouch back just touching the bottom of the zipper teeth. Stitch through all layers (pouch back, zipper, and lining) close to the folded edge of the pouch back. Fold the lining away from the zipper teeth and toward the wrong side of the pouch back, and press.

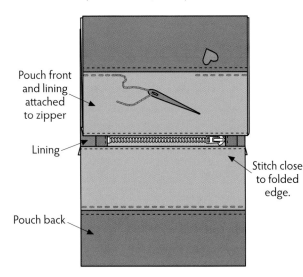

Pouch front and lining attached to zipper

Lining

Stitch close to folded edge.

Pouch back

FINISHING THE POUCH

1 Open the zipper half way. Pin the pouch front and back right sides together with raw edges aligned. Pin the lining right sides together with raw edges aligned. Make sure the seam allowances at the zipper are folded toward the pouch front and back, and away from the lining.

2 Using your regular presser foot and a ½" seam allowance, stitch all around the pouch, leaving a 4" opening at the bottom of the lining for turning. Press the seam allowances open.

3 To create the gusset at the bottom, clip the corners, and then open the seam allowances at one corner of the pouch and fold so that the

side seam is aligned with the bottom seam. Use a fabric-marking pen to draw a line perpendicular to the crease, 1" from the point. The line will be 2" long. Stitch along this line, and then trim the seam allowances to ½". Repeat with the second pouch corner and both lining corners.

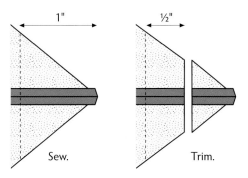

Sew.   Trim.

4 Turn the pouch right side out and open the zipper completely, but don't push the lining inside yet. Press the seam allowances to the inside at the opening in the lining, and hand or machine sew the opening closed. Then tuck the lining inside the pouch.

5 If desired, make a ribbon zipper pull. Fold a 5" length of ribbon in half, push the folded end through the zipper pull to make a small loop, and pull the two cut ends through the loop.

MAKING THE PINCUSHION TOP

1 With right sides together, align the 4½" edges of the linen 4½" x 4" rectangle and the print 4½" x 3" rectangle. Pin and sew the rectangles together using a ½" seam allowance. Press the seam allowances toward the print rectangle.

2 Topstitch close to the seam on the print fabric.

3 Place the felt heart on the print rectangle, leaving at least a 1" margin between the heart and the fabric raw edge, and pin. Hand sew the heart in place with embroidery floss or doubled sewing thread using an appliqué stitch.

4 Use a running stitch and three strands of embroidery floss to sew eleven rows of stitches on the linen, beginning ¼" from the print fabric, and continuing every ¼", so the last line of stitching is ¾" from the end.

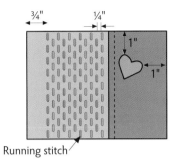

Running stitch

FINISHING THE PINCUSHION

1 Place the pincushion front right sides together with the linen 4½" x 6" rectangle. Pin the pieces in place, and sew them together using a ½" seam allowance, leaving a 2" opening on one side for turning.

2 Clip the corners and turn the pincushion right side out.

3 Fill the pincushion with stuffing until firm.

4 Hand sew the opening closed with a slipstitch.

▶ Raw-edge felt appliqué and hand embroidery combine to elevate an otherwise ordinary pincushion.

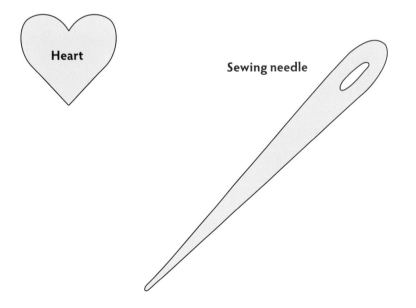

Heart

Sewing needle

Easy as Pie TEA TOWEL

I love pie almost as much as I love fabric, *especially fruit pie of any kind, and I simply couldn't resist making it the focus of this quirky tea towel. The appliqué is fused, and then finished with a zigzag edge—there's even a tiny bit of reverse appliqué thrown in for fun—and the embroidered words are just so cute!*

▶ **FINISHED TEA TOWEL:** 18" x 26"
▶ **TECHNIQUES:** Raw-edge fusible appliqué, reverse appliqué, and embroidery

MATERIALS

Yardage is based on 42"-wide fabric.

⅝ yard of natural linen or linen/cotton blend for tea towel
6" x 8" piece of light-yellow print for pie crust
5" x 7" piece of red print for pie filling
⅔ yard of ¼" mini pom-pom trim
All-purpose thread to match linen and cotton prints
Red pearl cotton thread, size 5
6" length of ½"-wide twill tape in color to match linen
¼ yard of 18"-wide fusible web
Water-soluble marker

CUTTING

From the linen, cut:
1 rectangle, 19½" x 27½"

EMBELLISHING THE TEA TOWEL

1 Trace the appliqué patterns on page 91 onto the paper side of the fusible web. Cut around each shape, leaving roughly a ¼" border, and fuse the web to the wrong side of the appliqué fabrics. Cut out each drawn shape, including the holes in the top crust.

2 Peel away the paper backing of the appliqué pieces and arrange the layers on the towel front, centering the pie horizontally and placing it 4¾" up from the bottom. Following the manufacturer's instructions, fuse the appliqués to the towel front. Using matching thread and a narrow zigzag or satin stitch, machine stitch the appliqués in place around the edges. Using a straight stitch, sew around the two reverse

appliqué openings. If desired, sew a decorative line to mark the edge of the top crust with a narrow zigzag or satin stitch.

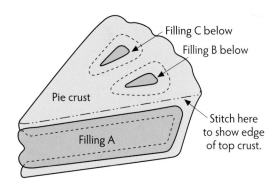

+ Change the Bobbin Thread

To make the stitching less visible on the back of the tea towel, use a thread that matches the towel fabric in the bobbin and a thread that matches the appliqué fabric in the top.

3 Trace the pattern for "Easy as" on page 91 onto the front of the tea towel with a water-soluble marker or other fabric-marking tool. Center the words above the pie, about 11" from the bottom of the towel. Embroider the words with the pearl cotton and a short running stitch. To avoid having a knot on the back of the towel, leave a long tail on the back when you start and stop stitching. When you finish embroidering, weave the tails through the backs of several adjacent stitches to secure the thread.

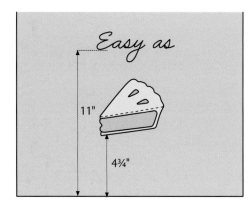

FINISHING THE TEA TOWEL

1 Turn under ⅜" along the sides of the tea towel and press. Turn under ⅜" again, press, and pin the hem.

2 Turn under ⅜" along the top and bottom edges and press. Turn under ⅜" again, press, and pin the hem.

3 Lay the tea towel wrong side up. In the upper left corner, mark the hem 3" to the right of the corner and 3" below the corner. Using these marks as a guide, cut a length of twill tape to fit under the hem from one mark to the other. Tuck the twill tape under the hem and pin it in place.

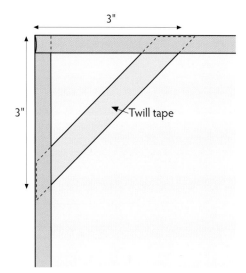

4 Using thread to match the linen, stitch ¼" from the edge around all sides, pivoting at the corners and backstitching at the end.

5 Lay the hemmed tea towel right side up. Pin the tape of the mini pom-pom trim to the towel, 2" from the bottom edge. Trim so that ½" of tape extends beyond each side. Tuck the extra ½" under at each side so the folded edge of the pom-pom tape is even with the side edges of the tea towel. Sew in place, using matching thread and a zipper foot, if needed.

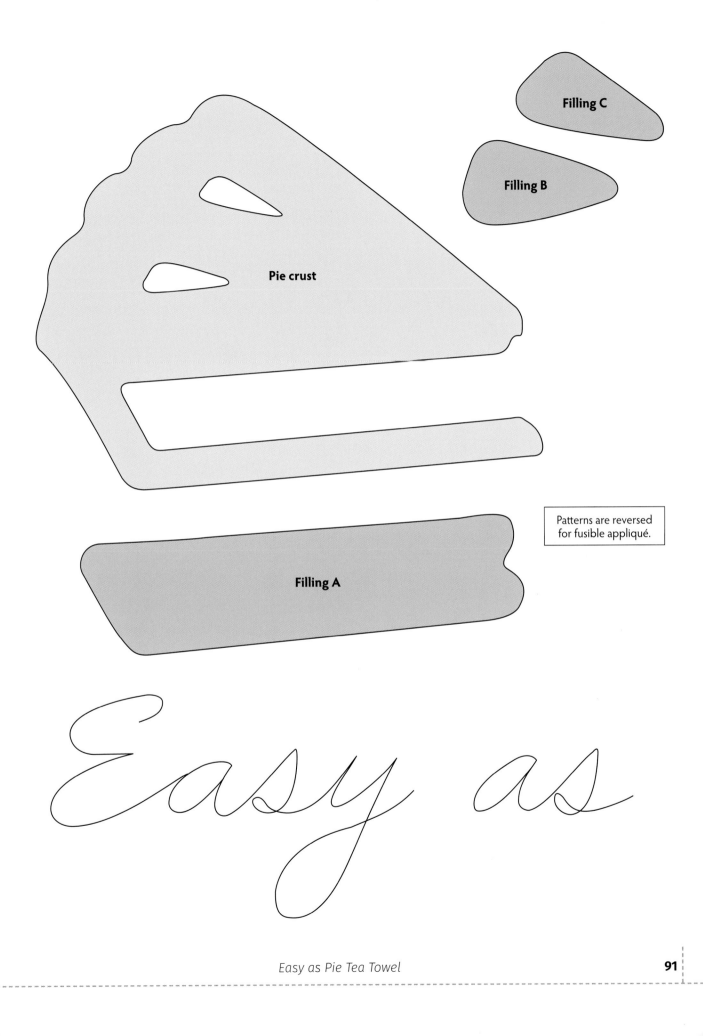

Filling C

Filling B

Pie crust

Patterns are reversed
for fusible appliqué.

Filling A

Easy as

No. 2 Pencil POUCH

The ubiquitous yellow No. 2 graphite pencil, with its convenient *attached eraser, is celebrated in this stylish pouch. Store your No. 2 pencils, or your more exotic colored pencils, art supplies, or school supplies in this quick-to-sew zippered bag.*

▶ **FINISHED POUCH:** 3½" x 9¾"
▶ **TECHNIQUE:** Raw-edge fusible appliqué

MATERIALS

Yardage is based on 42"-wide fabric.

¼ yard of blue cotton or linen/cotton blend
 solid for pouch
¼ yard of cotton print for lining
2" x 5" piece of yellow cotton solid or print
 for pencil length*
3" x 3" square of brown cotton solid for
 pencil point*
3" x 3" square of cotton stripe for eraser*
⅓ yard of 20"-wide lightweight fusible interfacing
3" x 5" piece of fusible web
9"-long zipper
Zipper foot

I used a yellow print for the pencil length, brown solid for the pencil tip, and a striped fabric that perfectly represented the eraser end.

CUTTING

From the blue solid, cut:
2 rectangles, 4½" x 10¾"
2 rectangles, 2" x 2¾"

From the cotton print, cut:
2 rectangles, 4¼" x 10¾"

From the interfacing, cut:
2 rectangles, 4" x 10¼"

EMBELLISHING THE POUCH

1 Referring to "Applying Fusible Interfacing" on page 15, fuse the interfacing to the blue 4½" x 10¾" rectangles.

2 Trace the pencil shapes onto the paper side of the fusible web, leaving at least ½" of space between each shape. Cut out each shape, leaving roughly a ¼" border. Following the manufacturer's instructions, fuse the shapes to the wrong side of the fabrics. Allow the fabric to cool, and then cut along the traced lines and remove the paper backing.

3 Lay one blue 4½" x 10¾" rectangle right side up. Position the appliqué shapes on the fabric so that the pencil is 1¼" from the side and bottom as shown. The pencil length should overlap the point and the eraser by about ¼".

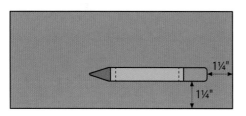

4 Following the manufacturer's instructions, fuse the pencil shapes in place.

5 With matching or contrasting thread, topstitch near the edges of the shapes. This is the pouch front.

PREPARING THE ZIPPER

1 Fold one blue 2" x 2¾" rectangle in half along the 2¾" length, wrong sides together, and press. Unfold the rectangle, fold each 2" raw edge toward the center, and press again. Fold in half once more and press to make one zipper tab, 2" x approximately ¾". Repeat with the second blue solid 2" x 2¾" rectangle.

2 Trim the extra tape at the starting end of the zipper just above the top of the zipper teeth, and at the end of the zipper so the remaining length is 9".

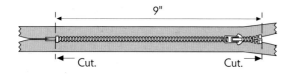

3 Place the bottom end of the zipper inside one of the folded zipper tabs, pushing it against the fold, and centering it. Topstitch close to the open edge of the zipper tab, catching all fabric layers and sewing straight across the zipper teeth to enclose the bottom end of the zipper. Open

the zipper by about 3" and repeat with the other zipper tab and the top of the zipper. Trim zipper tabs even with zipper tape.

ATTACHING THE ZIPPER

1 Fold the top edge of the pouch front ½" to the wrong side and press. Repeat with the pouch back. Set the two pieces aside.

2 Place one print 4½" x 10¾" lining piece right side up. Center the zipper on the lining along the top, 10¾"-long edge. With the zipper closed and the zipper pull to the right, align the top edge of the zipper tape with the raw edge of the lining and pin it in place. Using a zipper foot, baste the zipper to the lining close to the raw edge.

3 Place the lining piece right side up, with the zipper attached, so that the zipper side is toward you. Lay the pouch front on top of the zipper fabric with the folded edge of the pouch front just touching the bottom of the zipper teeth. With the zipper foot still attached, stitch through all layers (pouch front, zipper, and lining) close to the folded edge of the pouch front.

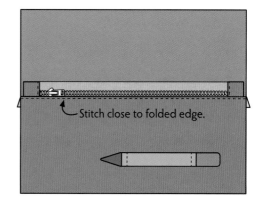

4 Fold the lining away from the zipper teeth and toward the wrong side of the pouch front. The wrong side of the lining will be facing the wrong side of the pouch front. Press.

5 Place the second lining piece right side up. Center the zipper (with the pouch front and lining attached) on the lining along the top, 10¾"-long edge. With the zipper closed and the zipper pull to the left, align the top edge of the zipper tape with the raw edge of the lining and pin it in place. Using a zipper foot, baste the zipper to the lining close to the raw edge.

Baste close to raw edge.

Lining ➝

Stitch close to folded edge.

Pouch front and lining attached to zipper

6 Place the lining piece right side up, with the zipper and pouch front attached, so that the zipper side is toward you. Lay the pouch back piece on top of the zipper fabric with the folded edge of the pouch front just touching the bottom of the zipper teeth. Stitch through all layers (pouch back, zipper, and lining) close to the folded edge of the pouch back. Fold the lining away from the zipper teeth and toward the wrong side of the pouch back, and press.

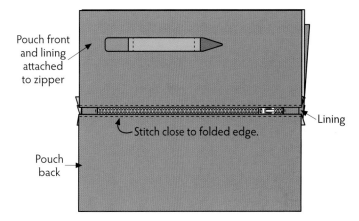

Pouch front and lining attached to zipper

Pouch back

Stitch close to folded edge.

Lining

FINISHING THE POUCH

1 Open the zipper half way. Pin the pouch front and back right sides together with raw edges aligned. Pin the lining right sides together with raw edges aligned. Make sure the seam allowances at the zipper are folded toward the pouch front and back, and away from the lining.

2 Using your regular presser foot and a ½" seam allowance, stitch all around, leaving a 4" opening at the bottom of the lining for turning.

3 Clip the bottom corners, turn the pouch right side out, and open the zipper completely, but don't tuck the lining inside yet. Press the seam allowances to the inside at the opening in the lining, and hand or machine sew the opening closed. Then tuck the lining inside the pouch.

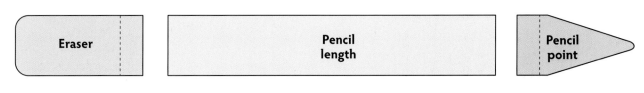

Eraser

Pencil length

Pencil point

+ Acknowledgments

Loads of thanks to the many people without whom this book wouldn't have been possible. Among those who provided invaluable advice and assistance, I'd like to, above all, extend my sincere gratitude to the following people:

▶ My husband, Jim, for his immense support and patience, even when the house is filled with piles of fabric and half-finished projects.

▶ My parents, who've always encouraged me to pursue my dreams and do what I love—my dad, my very first editor and a much better writer than me; and my mom, my enthusiastic cheerleader and a quilter long before I was.

▶ My talented friends of the Chicago Modern Quilt Guild, both in general, and also, particularly, those who generously agreed to test patterns. I'm so happy to have found "my people."

▶ All those at Martingale, for their hard work and vision, specifically, Karen Burns, for her encouragement and initial confidence in my talent; Ellen Pahl, for her meticulous attention to detail; Cathy Reitan, for gracefully managing my questions (and everything else!); Karen Soltys, for making it all happen; and, finally, the entire design team, for truly understanding my vision and putting together a top-notch book!

about the author

Amy Struckmeyer lives just outside of Chicago with her husband and their two strong-willed and creative children. Her love for textiles and making began early in her Waldorf School education with lessons in knitting, weaving, and sewing. An architect by profession, she now uses her design skills to create modern sewing projects and patterns, some of which have appeared in *Stitch* and *Modern Patchwork* magazines as well as the books *Sew Gifts!* and *Kitchen Stitches*. Visit her at FormWorkDesign.blogspot.com.